HABERMAS AND EUROPEAN
INTEGRATION

Manchester University Press

SHIVDEEP GREWAL

HABERMAS AND EUROPEAN INTEGRATION

Social and cultural modernity beyond the nation-state

MANCHESTER UNIVERSITY PRESS

The right of Shivdeep Grewal to be identified as the author of this work has been asserted by him in accordance with the Copyright, Designs and Patents Act 1988.

The publisher has no responsibility for the persistence or accuracy of URLs for any external or third-party internet websites referred to in this book, and does not guarantee that any content on such websites is, or will remain, accurate or appropriate.

Published by Manchester University Press
Altrincham Street, Manchester M1 7JA, UK
www.manchesteruniversitypress.co.uk

British Library Cataloguing-in-Publication Data is available

ISBN   978 1 5261 4273 3   paperback

This edition first published by Manchester University Press 2019

CONTENTS

Figures and Tables

Figures

Tables

PREFACE AND ACKNOWLEDGEMENTS

This study builds on research conducted at the Universities of Reading and Essex, yet its origins lie further back. As an undergraduate, I studied English Literature. The critics impressed me as much as the writers, and it would not be inaccurate to say that my work to date has been marked by early readings of Susan Sontag and Marshall McLuhan, the French poststructuralists and the Frankfurt School. My attention soon turned to the work of Jürgen Habermas. I was inspired by the affirmative account of modernity at its heart. This has been the object of critique for some time, and in recent years it has seemed difficult even to articulate. That it remains plausible to me, still – despite everything, a declaration of hope – is the reason I have persisted with the present avenue of research.

I had originally intended to produce an account of the 'democratic deficit'. This would have been structured by a selection of Habermas's concepts, particularly those of his later, legal-democratic, theory. After the tragic events of 9/11, however, I was forced, like many others, to question my most basic assumptions. It gradually became apparent that Habermas's work was not rendered obsolete by the dramatic occurrences of the time, which in a sense marked the passing of the postwar context in which he had developed his major ideas. I would have to broaden my investigation, I realised, not abandon it.

Habermas has written of the 'densely populated, ethnically mixed suburbs in the vicinity of Heathrow Airport' (2001c: 75). I grew up nearby, and it was to the suburbs that I returned to do the bulk of the writing. More than once a key sentence or idea has come to me on an evening stroll (in unconscious homage to Walter Benjamin, perhaps), and the importance to my research of the European 'lifeworld', the experiential rather than market-administrative aspect of the integration process, probably stems from this peripatetic orientation. I also worked in the vicinity of Heathrow Airport, as a visiting lecturer at Brunel University – my warmest gratitude goes to Professors Justin Fisher and Alex Warleigh-Lack for inviting me back each year.

Thanks are due to a number of people. To begin with, Professor Richard Bellamy – I could not have asked for a better supervisor. My gratitude also goes to Professor Emil Kirchner and Professor William Outhwaite, both in relation to this study and the research that preceded it. Along with everyone at Manchester University Press, I am indebted to Professor Thomas

Christiansen for his positive early comments. I am also grateful to the anonymous reviewer for a supportive response to my initial proposal. Parts of this study appeared in *Politics*, the *Journal of European Integration* and the *Journal of European Public Policy*; reprint permissions granted by Blackwell, Routledge, Polity and Suhrkamp are gratefully acknowledged. Finally, I would like to thank Professor Habermas, whose words of encouragement came at the perfect time.

Reclining in a wicker chair in Bangkok, I began reading William Gibson's *Neuromancer* (1984). I was somewhat encouraged to learn that the author had completed it at the grand old age of thirty-six, and that I therefore had twelve solid years to produce a comparable work of my own. It remains unwritten. The engagement with geopolitics and philosophy that seemed a prerequisite for the task was compelling in itself, and, twelve years on, this study exists in place of the envisaged novel, though the worldviews of Habermas and Gibson are, of course, quite different. Another work notable for its prescience is John Goff's *The Last Days of the Most Hidden Man* (1992). He has kindly contributed an afterword.

Finally, I am grateful to my family and friends, who have been with me through so many challenging times. If I began to list them all, and the debts of gratitude I owe, this preface would run to a volume in itself.

Shivdeep Grewal
London

Habermas and European integration was published in 2012. A couple of months later, European Central Bank president Mario Draghi stated the commitment 'to do whatever it takes to preserve the euro'. Completed during the crisis that had afflicted the eurozone since 2009, the book bears the imprint of the time. A tone of existential questioning entered mainstream discussion of the European project. It has lingered in the background ever since.

The second edition is due for release in the summer of 2019. Like the first, a crisis precedes it. The year 2015 saw major terrorist attacks in France.[1] Occurring in January and November,[2] these formed parentheses around the shift of asylum policy initiated by German chancellor Angela Merkel in response to the Syrian civil war. For Jürgen Habermas, this combination of events signified the need for 'a much closer sense of co-operation and solidarity than anything European nations, even those tied up to one another in the currency union, have so far managed to achieve' (2015e). The political turbulence was exacerbated by economic strains that had accumulated since 2009.[3]

The effects of the two crises have been somewhat mixed. The implications continue to unfold. Brexit, on the one hand, and the rise of Emmanuel Macron, on the other, can be argued for as consequences. The failure to conclude the Article 50 process in March 2019 and the European Parliament elections of May presage numerous conceivable futures.

How does the book relate to the present conjuncture? At its core is Habermas's conception of the European Union (EU). This conception remains essentially unchanged, as will be evident from the survey of his recent work undertaken in the pages that follow. Moreover, its 'explanatory power' in the face of the disparate and often contradictory dynamics at play in contemporary Europe remains without parallel in the domain of social theory.

Beginning with Habermas's political writings and working back from these to his theoretical ones distinguished this book from much of the scholarship in the field. In general, it had not been the practice to emphasise the socio-political matrix within which his successive scholarly publications were conceived and shaped. Major works such as *The Theory of Communicative Action* (TCA), *The Philosophical Discourse of Modernity* (PDM), *Between Facts and Norms* (BFN), and *The Structural Transformation of the Public Sphere* can be viewed as responses – at turns descriptive and prescriptive, sober and cautiously optimistic – to shifting historical realities, rather than products of cloistered intellection. In turn, the echoes of these responses have continued to reverberate in Habermas's political writings, sometimes within the space of a single article.

I have tried to do justice to the scope of Habermas's thinking on Europe, its capacity to deal simultaneously with the widest array of developments. This 'panoramic' traversal of concepts and events gives the book its particular form and style – so too does the cognitive shift brought about by the internet, the inclination to follow a line of thought associatively across multiple contexts. The internet also has the capacity to fragment and disperse knowledge, notes Habermas (2014). Rather than revel in this 'centrifugal' tendency (a mode of delirious resignation common today), I have attempted to follow him in showing that contemporary reality – at once virtual and embodied – can still be subject to a 'scientifically informed enlightenment', a process of philosophical reflection that 'none of the pertinent scientific disciplines – neither economics nor political science or sociology – can, in and of themselves, provide' (Habermas, 2015d).

By writing on Habermas's work I hoped to broaden its appeal. Scholars engaged mainly with the legal-democratic concepts of BFN have developed a rich and sophisticated literature on the EU. By its very nature, however, this literature speaks only to students, academics and specialists. The work of Habermas's poststructuralist peers – and Bruno Latour, in particular – has continued, meanwhile, to inspire philosophical initiatives outside academia, despite predictions of a fall into obscurity with *l'affaire Sokal*.[4] Perhaps unintentionally, the nihilism of these milieux has resonated with sections of the 'alt-right'.

Creative engagement with Habermas's work would appear, by contrast, to have reached a plateau. This has perhaps been due to the reverence of his dedicated readers. While sharing this reverence, I have been concerned to bring Habermas's thought into engagement with the disharmonies of contemporary politics, and, in particular, the contexts of urban experience in which these disharmonies are embedded – in the latter regard, I have learned much from Natsuo Kirino and J.G. Ballard, among other 'writers of social science' (see Appendix), and from a renewed engagement with Habermas's *Knowledge and Human Interests* (1968), its consideration of positivism of renewed significance. My goal has been to suggest a deeper and somewhat 'grittier' approach than those that developed in the context of the 'Third Way'.[5]

Habermas's conception of democracy within the modern state straddles TCA and BFN, though this is not always acknowledged. Partiality is shown not only by legal-minded enthusiasts for the latter: critics of 'lifeworld colonisation' stemming from EU juridification have looked to TCA while disputing potentials for the supranational consolidation of democracy, and the capacity of law to effect this. I have tried to avoid the shortcomings of both perspectives.

TCA identifies pathologies in the spheres of culture and individual psychology that result when administrative and economic imperatives colonise the lifeworld of everyday interaction. Not commonly associated with the democratic deficit, phenomena such as the 'unsettling of collective identity' and 'alienation' are brought within the scope of analysis.

Habermas and European integration considered two roughly contemporary developments. Dutch Eurosceptic Pim Fortuyn was discussed in relation to the end of the 'permissive consensus' on European integration, the democratic deficit ceasing at last to be amelliorable by means of the welfare state and consumerism. Also discussed was the burgeoning significance of information technology, both in relation to individuals and states – this was understood to promote an *intensification* of lifeworld colonisation.[6] The two developments were examined separately: a significant overlap between them was not proposed. The present political context in Europe, and across the world, is quite different, with social media in a sense *constituting* populism (Habermas, 2016a). Occurring prior to the founding of Facebook in 2004, Youtube in 2005, and Twitter in 2006, Fortuyn's short political career lacked the social media basis of recent populist mobilisations. Writing of Brexit, by contrast, Habermas employed the vocabulary of TCA to describe the role of information technology and lifeworld colonisation (Habermas, 2016a; see also Outhwaite, 2017).

In the post-Snowden era, the sense of living under the conditions of an 'information war', the battlefield often that of interpersonal relations, is pervasive.[7] TCA's capacity to inform thinking on the socially and politically corrosive effects of social media is, therefore, of relevance to the study of democracy in Europe, helping to discern a terrain of conflict that transgresses private and public spheres, and distinctions between domestic politics and international relations.

In terms of the account of 'cultural modernity' outlined in the first edition of *Habermas and European integration*, the decline of American neoconservatism has coincided with the rise of the alt-right.[8] In the parlance of chapter 7 (see figure 7.3, in particular), the latter might be thought of as a fusion of 'consumerist populism', as exemplified by Pim Fortuyn, with phenomena such as 'counter Enlightenment radicalism' and 'esotericism'. The consequent emergence of 'authoritarian populism'[9] as an ideological formation owes much to the conflation of antimodern perspectives facilitated by the internet.[10]

Habermas has continued to elaborate themes from BFN in the years since the eurozone crisis. Potentials exist, he suggests, not only for the erosion but also the supranational consolidation of welfare state democracy.[11] In *The Lure of Technocracy* (2013), he emphasises the distinctness of the political entity that would come into being in the event of a further push for integration by a core of eurozone states. This would not entail a move from a confederal structure to a properly federal one but a more innovative arrangement. For this 'supra-national democracy' would break with the classical notion of sovereignty by having a 'joint fiscal, budgetary and economic policy, and especially with a harmonization of social policy', while, at the same time, preserving states' 'monopoly on the legitimate use of force', 'their function as the implement-ing administrations', and their status as the 'final custodians of civil liberties' (Habermas, 2015a: 14).

Thus, the envisaged path of state-formation

> cannot be understood on the model of a two-stage process according to which the political processes within the constituted polity are based on the constitution of the state powers. A more appropriate model is instead a three-stage one which already presupposes the existence of democratically constituted nation-states. (Habermas, 2017a: 181)

An arrangement of this sort, geared to preserving the normative status quo of constituent nation-states (particularly in the area of social policy), would require a means for them all, irrespective of size, to defend their historic achievements against supranational encroachments. Though voters already have, in effect, the dual identities of European and member state citizens, it would require a disproportionate assertion of the latter to defend social rights. Significantly, a basis for this 'preservative' exercise of power is already present in the Lisbon Treaty, Habermas notes, for the currently

> degressive proportional allocation of seats in the European Parliament [which privileges smaller member states] can be justified democratically on the grounds that each of the national peoples involved in the constitution-building process wishes to keep open the possibility of lending its national interests greater weight if need be not only via the decisions of the Council, but also on a case-by-case basis in the negotiations and votes of the Parliament. (Habermas, 2017a: 179)

Despite these democratic potentials, however, Habermas has recently underscored the risk of the eurozone being consolidated without addressing the divergence in fortunes between its northern and southern members (Habermas, 2018c).

> A democratic eurozone doesn't just need to be made "weatherproof" against speculation – by way of a banking union, a corresponding insolvency procedure, a joint deposit insurance scheme and an EU-level monetary fund. More than anything, it must be outfitted with sufficient competencies and budgetary means to intervene to keep the member states from further drifting apart economically and socially. It's not just about fiscal stabilization, but about convergence – the credible political intent of the economically and politically strongest member states to fulfill the common currency's broken promise of convergent economic developments. (Habermas, 2018b)

Since his ascent to the presidency of France in 2017, Emmanuel Macron has been praised by Habermas for his passionate advocacy of the European project (2017b), particularly the ideals of social and economic convergence referred to above. Though he has questioned the composition of Macron's programme, expressing the hope that 'he is at least a convinced left-leaning liberal' (2018a), and emphasising that he 'is rightly criticized in his own country for the socially imbalanced nature of his reforms' (2018b), Habermas's overall assessment has been clear: 'Seldom have the contingencies of history emerged so prominently than with the unexpected rise of this fascinating – perhaps blindingly so, in any case extraordinary – person' (2017c).

To some extent, then, Macron would seem the embodiment of Habermas's ideals. Furthermore, the empirical assertion put forward in the first edition of this book that Habermas's vision for Europe was too 'idiosyncratic' (see page 8) to unite social democrats and the radical left has lost some of its validity since Macron's victory. This shift is a legacy of the eurozone crisis: if the fault lines of the radical left on the European question were once quite obscure, the Greek debt crisis brought tensions between outright Eurosceptics and cautious Europeanists, such as former Syriza Minster of Finance Yanis Varoufakis, to the fore. The extraordinary pressures of the crisis would seem to have forged a Europhile tendency on the left – indeed, Varoufakis (2017) praised Macron, and urged the French left to back him, largely on the grounds that he had been sympathetic to the Greek cause at the time.[12]

Conversely, Macron might be said to have foundered when he has stressed elements of his political vision at odds with that of Habermas. Having come to power through a vigorous and direct engagement with the electorate, he retreated from view after victory, ostensibly to concentrate on the implementation of his ambitious programme. This 'Jupiterian' stance, and a series of utterances which equated him in the public mind with aloofness and elitism, brought to the fore orientations that were there at the outset. Indeed, Habermas drew attention early on to Macron's comfort with the aesthetics of state power, recalling – albeit lightheartedly – 'Carl Schmitt's nostalgic view ... [of] the French counter-enlightenment of the 19th century' (2017c).[13] Similarly, in conveying his orientation towards Europe, Macron broached comparison not only with Charles de Gaulle, but also with François Mitterrand, the latter's eulogising of Ernst Jünger[14] recalling Macron's – highly qualified – praise for Philippe Pétain.

Nor were these merely aesthetic preferences, for Macron's project rests on a distinct *philosophical* outlook, interesting both for its commonalities and divergences with that of Habermas. Macron's debt to French philosopher Paul Ricoeur (Humphreys, 2017), particularly the latter's somewhat favourable view of ideology (as distinct from Habermas's concern with emancipation), is significant in this regard:

> post-modernism was the worst thing that could have happened to our democracy. The idea that you have to deconstruct and destroy all grand narratives is not a good one. (Macron, 2017)

This criticism of the poststructuralists – and Lyotard (1979), in particular – might seem of a piece with PDM. Yet Macron's consequent stratagem – to counter the myths of authoritarian populism with myths from the symbolic reservoir of European history – left little space for dialogue. His preference for ideology to democratic engagement, combined with unpopular economic reforms, gave rise to the *gilets jaunes* movement, its sudden mobilisations, organised almost entirely online, harrying his presidency in the closing months of 2018. In the end, only a carefully worded address to the nation, watched by 23 million television viewers, would begin to quell the disturbances (Macron, 2018). Since then, a nation-wide consultation, *le grand débat*, has been launched with the intention of reinvigorating French democracy, allowing Macron to regain at least some of the popularity that brought him to office. This approach has been praised by François Bayrou as heralding a new era, the marriage of social justice with economic progress (BBC News, 2018).

Shivdeep Grewal
London

Notes

1 By a macabre coincidence, Michel Houellebecq's novel *Soumission* (2015), which details the victory of a Muslim candidate in the French presidential elections of 2022, was published on 7 January 2015, the same day as the attack by Islamist militants at the Paris headquarters of the satirical magazine *Charlie Hebdo*. Soon a bestseller, the novel contributed further to the author's profound entanglement with the culture and politics of France and western Europe. The introductory chapter of *Habermas and European integration* opens with a quote from Habermas, while the concluding chapter opens with a quote from Houellebecq. In this way, I sought to juxtapose the most significant intellectual currents of the time, precursors of the contending cosmopolitans and authoritarian populists of the present day. Only later did it occur to me that both quotes dated, in their original publications, from 1998 – in the ensuing two decades, Habermas alone has offered a sufficiently powerful and sophisticated alternative to Houellebecq's theses, going beyond politics to deal with themes as diverse as genetic engineering (2003), free will (2013a), and the continuing importance of philosophy in the form of critical social theory (2015d).
2 See Habermas (2015e).
3 See Genna and Wilson (2016).
4 Houellebecq (1998) was among those wrong-footed, poststructuralist thinkers read by a new generation in relation to 'hauntology', 'capitalist realism', 'accelerationism', 'speculative realism' and 'cosmic pessimism'. Indeed, a shared interest of these constituencies has been the 'weird' ontologies of H.P. Lovecraft, going beyond Houellebecq's (1991) essentially biographical treatment of the latter.
5 The online news resource Eurointelligence has been a source of inspiration, offering a welcome alternative to the state-centrism of contemporaries such as Stratfor. Reductionism of the latter's sort often conceals an ignorance of EU politics. The *sui generis* character of the EU is, by contrast, a central tenet of this book.
6 Shoshana Zuboff's (2019) research provides a formidable empirical resource for this

line of reasoning. Of particular interest is her distinction of a new 'instrumentarian' form of power from the 'totalitarian' variants of the previous century.

7   One recalls the cavalier manner in which a prominent Tory politician, interviewed during the live BBC Television referendum broadcast, employed the term 'psy-ops' when discussing the strategy of his 'Vote Leave' campaign colleagues, and the deepening – indeed, *metaphysical* – unease, to this day not dispelled, that a coup had transpired somewhat by accident. In terms of perturbations to the public sphere, an analogy might be drawn between the propaganda bombardment of the referendum campaign and the turbulence of financial markets during the eurozone crisis.

8   See Sloterdijk (2016) for a critique of populism sympathetic to American neoconservatives.

9   See Habermas (2016b).

10 The complexion of 'Occidental dandyism' has passed through various iterations in the present decade (see, for example, McLemee, 2011 and Kriss, 2017). With regard to ideological progenitors, a productive path of research might progress from *Der Stürmer* and *Bagatelles pour un massacre* to *Bo' Selecta* and Breitbart News, the use of surreal imagery and grotesquery a feature of populist discourse to the present day. In the latter regard, it might be asked whether studies grounded in political science and political theory, which have, unsurprisingly, proliferated in recent years, are equipped to access and explicate the experiential core of populism as well as, say, Luc Tuymans' (2016) curatorial discussion of James Ensor's work, where the concept of 'bliss' is brought to the fore.

In keeping with the first edition of *Habermas and European integration*, contemporary literature may be drawn on to illuminate the political landscape. Ballard is particularly relevant in this regard, his outlook indebted strongly to Surrealism. With regard to Brexit, Ballard's novel *Kingdom Come* (2006) proved uncannily prescient, anticipating by a decade the shift from consumerist to authoritarian populism that characterised the referendum campaign. Ballard portrayed the accompanying 'bliss' of moral and political degeneration, the disregard for form (both social and aesthetic) and the progressive dissolution of class distinctions, recalling at times Hannah Arendt's *The Origins of Totalitarianism* (1951). The degradation of language, as discussed by George Steiner (1964) in relation to Nazism, is also captured, though perhaps unwittingly, by Ballard: the critical consensus on *Kingdom Come* was that the novel marked a stylistic low point for the author, yet this lapse into indifferent prose would seem, in retrospect, to anticipate the intellectual decay that has been prevalent since its publication – a comparable argument might be made for Roberto Bolaño's *2666* (2004).

11 Despite the disquieting headlines, European integration continues apace. One might consider the 'classic case of state formation' at work in the ECJ's recent injunction to halt the replacement of supreme court judges in Poland (Eurointelligence, 2018), or the signing of the Aachen Treaty, with its promise of intensified Franco-German cooperation.

12 Even Varoufakis's (2018) recent criticisms of Macron lament the perceived failure of his project, which is blamed on German self-interest, rather than the goals of the project itself. Habermas's (2015ac) exchange with political economist Wolfgang Streeck (2014, 2017), meanwhile, gives a sense of the distinctness in perspectives between the former and many on the Marxian left. The attitudes of this constituency had hardened, and their orientation to the nation-state become more strident and programmatic, in response to the tensions between Greece and Germany during the eurozone crisis (see Habermas, 2015bc). Striking a sombre note, Habermas had argued that the 'European parties on the Left are set to repeat their historical error of 1914' (2015a: 102), and has continued, more recently, to criticise what he sees as the

'self-satisfied anti-capitalism of the left-wing nationalists' (2017c). With regard to Streeck, in particular, Habermas argued that

> the case for a return to the format of small nation states is not evident to me. For these would have to be run on globalised markets on the same lines as global conglomerates. That would signify a complete abdication of politics in the face of the imperatives of unregulated markets. (2016a)

For thoughtful reflection on Streeck's nationalism, see Chakrabortty (2016). John Gray's (2016) accomodation to populism has been more straightforwardly abject.

13   Macron's conception of sovereignty (Habermas, 2017c) might be assessed in relation to that of Carl Schmitt (1922).

14   The role of the writer in the European project calls for further study. See, for example, Bailey (2016) on Thomas Mann.

*A*BBREVIATIONS

BFN	*Between Facts and Norms: Contributions to a Discourse Theory of Law and Democracy*
BEUC	European Office of Consumer Unions
CEPLIS	Conseil Européen des Professions Libérales
CLS	Council Legal Service
COMECON	Council for Mutual Economic Assistance
COREPER	Committee of Permanent Representatives
DG	Directorate General (a department of the European Commission)
EC	European Community
ECJ	European Court of Justice
EMCEF	European Federation of Chemical and General Workers' Unions
EMU	European Monetary Union
EP	European Parliament
EPP-ED	European People's Party
EPU	European Political Union
ESC	Economic and Social Committee
ESM	European Social Model
ETUC/ETUI	European Trade Union Confederation/European Trade Union Institute
EU	European Union
EUW	European Union of Women
FEANTSA	European Federation of Organisations Working with the Homeless
FRG	Federal Republic of Germany
GMB	General, Municipal, Boilermakers and Allied Trades Union
GUE-NGL	Group of the United European Left/Nordic Green Left
MEP	Member of the European Parliament
MLG	Multi-level governance
NATO	North Atlantic Treaty Organisation
NGO	Non-Governmental Organisation
NSM	New Social Movement
PDM	*The Philosophical Discourse of Modernity: Twelve Lectures*
PES	Party of European Socialists
SEA	Single European Act
TCA	*The Theory of Communicative Action* (Volumes I and II)

TEU   Treaty on European Union (also known as the Maastricht Treaty)
UNICE   Union of Industrial and Employers' Confederations

Introduction

Modernity, welfare state and EUtopia

"Flow and boundary" – a suggestive image for a new constellation of border crossings.   —Habermas, 1998[1]

From its conception to the referenda of 2005 where it met its end, German philosopher Jürgen Habermas wrote in support of the European Constitution. An account of his efforts must, however, be more than a catalogue of texts. For his status as the last of the great system builders of European philosophy, comparable with Hegel in the breadth and explanatory power of his thought, precludes a straightforward approach of this type. If it is to do justice to its subject matter, such a work must also consider the ways in which Habermas's political writings have *modified*, albeit subtly, his social and legal-democratic theory, yielding in the process a distinctive conception of the European Union (EU). The aim of this study is the delineation of this conception, its application and critique.

This avenue of research has antecedents. A decade ago, Bellamy and Castiglione (2000b) wrote of a conceptual shift in the field of EU studies, a 'normative turn' prompted by specific theoretical and political developments. In the theoretical case, the impetus came initially from the constructivist wing of International Relations scholarship. The unravelling, since Maastricht, of the 'permissive consensus' – a perception of European integration as an innocuously technical, rather than political, endeavour – also impelled a deeper consideration of norms. Debate centred here on which institutional and constitutional arrangements might be capable of fostering much-needed legitimacy.

Habermas participated directly in the latter debate (Habermas, 2001a, 2005). His social and legal-democratic theory also exerted an appreciable, if implicit, influence on constructivist streams of thought. The groundbreaking work of Eriksen and Fossum (2000; Eriksen, 2005, 2009) provides the most developed Habermasian account of the EU to date.

This study brings the phenomenological aspect of Habermas's thought to the normative turn. Attention is given to the consequences for the everyday 'lifeworld' of the integration process. An experiential counterpart to its political and economic dimensions is therefore presumed.

Also taken seriously is the intellectual context in which the Constitution developed. The deepening of 'cultural pessimism' (McCarthy, 1997: vii) in the wake of 9/11 had the effect of marginalising Habermas's ideas, though without entirely discrediting the Enlightenment tradition that had inspired them. Rather, it was the *polarisation* between instrumentalist variants of Enlightenment thinking, of the sort Horkheimer and Adorno (2002: 1) had traced to Francis Bacon, on the one hand, and positions inherently sceptical of reason, on the other, that detracted from Habermas's subtler interventions.[2]

The Anglo-American Enlightenment exceeded its Continental counterpart in popularity at this time. Along with a favourable geopolitical configuration, American neoconservatives benefited from this state of affairs, to the point of military intervention in Iraq being couched by them in terms evocative of the American Revolution and the Declaration of Independence of 1776. Irrespective of their appropriateness, the rhetorical force of these analogies generally exceeded that of arguments in favour of the European Constitution, though French President Jacques Chirac did describe the latter as the 'daughter' of the Revolution of 1789. There were refusals, too, both esoteric and populist, of Enlightenment progressivism. The proponents could be distinguished equally from the neoconservatives and Habermas's Cosmopolitan stance.

Writing of this period, Bernard-Henri Lévy argued that Paris had ceded its status as the 'world capital of intellectual discussion' to New York (2007: 1), with commentators such as Christopher Hitchens now setting the agenda. A corresponding drift toward punditry and contrarianism served further to obscure Habermas's painstaking navigation between philosophical traditions. While impeding its reception in the mediasphere, however, the dialectical form of his thought can help to illuminate the era of the European Constitution, and, beyond that political and intellectual palimpsest, the world that has come to replace it.

Modernity

Given their variety, Outhwaite (1996: 3) suggests 'modernity' as a useful 'organising category' for Habermas's writings. The term links the latter's journalistic and theoretical works, providing a thread of continuity that has run through both since the early 1960s. Modernity is also the cautiously utopian ideal that has motivated his political prescriptions. Indeed, while conceding its shortcomings, as identified by critics from across the political spectrum, Habermas (1996a) has argued for it as an 'unfinished' project, its 'highly conditional promise of autonomy, justice, democracy, and solidarity' as yet to be redeemed (Outhwaite, 1996: 3).

The impasse faced by modernity – identified variously with postmodernism, 'The end of history' (Fukuyama, 1989), *The Clash of Civilisations* (Huntington, 1996), etc. – stems, Habermas suggests, from adherence to outdated conceptual forms, forms in terms of which it has hitherto been conceived. Most prominent among these has been the rational human subject, as considered by thinkers such as Descartes and Kant. While contributing to its critique, however, Habermas has been at pains to defend the conception of reason associated with this subject. Hence, he has resisted both the wholesale disavowal of reason, as associated with French poststructuralism, and its attenuation into the 'strategic-instrumental' form characteristic of, for example, rational choice theory. At the same time, he has declined to locate rationality in macrosubjects – such as the nation, working class or 'social system' – arguing, instead, for an 'intersubjective' conception of it. Rationality is to be found in the phenomenological lifeworld of social interaction, a reservoir of shared cultural knowledge, traditions and affiliations (Habermas, 1995, 1997a). Against the phenomenology of Husserl, Habermas considers language to be central to the constitution of the lifeworld and its capacity to renew itself over time. Indeed, it is in the very *structure* of linguistic interaction that the 'communicative rationality' of the lifeworld is thought by him to reside. The aim of his theoretical work has been to overcome the limitations that confront subject-centred conceptions of rationality, with the lifeworld bridging the gap between, otherwise monadic, individuals or collectives.

Given these assumptions, it is understandable why democratisation of the EU has been viewed by Habermas as important. Lacking the bedrock of tradition as a source of legitimacy, the process of European integration would seem to necessitate the consultation and deliberation of citizens, and hence the assertion of communicative rationality, if popular acceptance is to be attained. In theory at least, democratisation would contribute to the transcendence of another conceptual impasse regarded by Habermas as impeding modernity: the 'aporia' of the nation-state.

Habermas has distinguished between *social modernity* and *cultural modernity* (Habermas, 1994b: 28). Social modernity can be understood as the historical struggle of the lifeworld to resist, and perhaps reverse, its 'colonisation' (Habermas, 1995) by economic and administrative imperatives, a contest that culminated in the twentieth-century with the birth of the welfare state (Ashenden, 1998: 120). Habermas's article (2001a) on a constitution for the EU suggests the continuation of social modernity, particularly lifeworld colonisation, at the continental level. The EU is looked to as a guarantor, in the face of transnational markets, of the 'European way of life' (Jospin cited in Habermas, 2001a: 9) made possible in the postwar era by the welfare state. Indeed, one of Habermas's central claims is that the meaningful exercise of democratic citizenship requires sufficient levels of social welfare (Ashenden, 1998: 125), in the absence of which the rationality potential of the lifeworld may lie dormant or may even regress. The American Social Model has featured in Habermas's journalistic writings as a warning of the possible future for Europe in the event that its comparatively generous welfare levels were not maintained. Nevertheless, in depicting the EU primarily as a vehicle for modernity, Habermas's ideas are not as straightforwardly social demo- cratic as his defence of the welfare state would suggest.

The social modernity approach would not be out of place in the existing corpus of integration theory. For the latter, too, is concerned with the devel- opmental logics of administrations and markets. However, the *telos* of integration in a particular policy area would remain to be accounted for: the *relationship* between domestic and supranational levels is a 'vertical' dialectic foreign to Habermas's thought, with its emphasis on the 'horizontal' trajec- tories of national administrations. A range of integration theories will be drawn on with a view to augmenting the social modernity approach.

In the course of this study, particular attention is paid to the area of social policy. There are two reasons for this. First, the welfare state is thought of by Habermas as the culmination of social modernity. Second, he has suggested that policy making in this area is informed by an economistic view of life, of which lifeworld colonisation is ultimately the consequence (Habermas, 1994c, 1995). Hence, social policy may actually obstruct one of the promises of modernity: the liberation of the lifeworld from the strictures of economistic reasoning.

Cultural modernity concerns the discourses and traditions constitutive of the lifeworld. In premodern cultures, 'religio-metaphysical' worldviews formed the normative core of the lifeworld. In the West, these worldviews began to dissolve with the onset of modernity, a process described by Weber as 'disenchantment'. Modernity would increasingly have to draw on itself for norms.[3] The term 'rationalisation' denotes the ensuing separation of the substantive reason previously locked into these worldviews into three 'moments' or 'value spheres'. With time, each became institutionalised, giving rise to the 'expert cultures' of science and knowledge, morality and law and artistic practice and criticism (Habermas, 1996a, 1997a, 1998a).

While Weber equated disenchantment with a pervasive loss of meaning (Habermas, 1997a: xix), Habermas has greeted the rationalisation it gives rise to more positively. If allowed to follow its inherent logics, he argues, rationalisation would free the lifeworld to establish its normative core on the basis of dialogue, with the specialised resources of each value sphere drawn on freely in the course of public discussion. Yet, in his view, ratio- nalisation has been obstructed in the West through the enduring influence of nationalism, consumerism and varieties of economistic thinking – the latter referred to as 'productivism' (Habermas, 1996b: 9) – which together perform the role once alloted to religio-metaphysical worldviews: the provi- sion of norms for the coordination of social life (White, 1990: 117). Encouraging signs of cultural modernity have, for Habermas, been discern- able during important European summits, when the outlines of a transnational public sphere were visible, with citizens momentarily recognising a host of shared concerns (Müller, 2001).

A hermeneutics of integration

This study engages with Habermas's thought as a totality, though attention is focussed on themes such as communicative rationality that began to surface in the 1970s (White, 1990: 1). The aim is to avoid taking elements of his work in isolation and simply extrapolating these to the level of the EU. In relation to Marxism, Outhwaite (1996: 9) identified such 'asset stripping' with Schumpeter and Dahrendorf. Something similar has characterised commentary on Habermas's turn to Europe: identified with the tradition of Polanyi and Scharpf, he is subsequently judged as a lapsed social democrat (Grewal, 2010).[4] The situation recalls one written of by Puchala (1972) several decades ago. Scholars of international integration, he suggested, resembled the blind men who, according to an Indian folktale, sought to ascertain an elephant's appearance by touch alone. Unsurprisingly, both scholars and blindmen, extrapolating from the aspects of the 'beast' closest to hand, were mistaken in their comprehension of the whole. This study aims to forestall such confusion in relation to Habermas's conception of the EU.

The approach taken here is termed a 'hermeneutics of integration' (Grewal, 2005: 194). It calls for the interpretation of a given policy context or historical conjuncture as whole, ranging widely over its political, economic and cultural dimensions, with the EU taken as the appropriate level of analysis for this endeavour.

Laying the basis for this approach called for attention to Habermas's journalism, understood here as those works, or moments in works, that have addressed or attempted to shape political tendencies or events. The challenge has been to work within the arc of Habermas's thought in order to salvage an account of the EU that was, albeit implicitly, *there already*, rather than fabricating such an account *ex nihilo*. Reading the journalism chronologically, with an emphasis on work from the late 1970s onwards, is quite different to the approach that is usually taken, the foregrounding of Habermas's theoretical writings.

Motifs of social and cultural modernity recur in Habermas's journalism. In the case of social modernity, suggestions of 'juridification', the legal consolidation of successive stages of social evolution, surfaced repeatedly in relation to both the nation-state and EU. Also common were allusions to the 'reflective welfare state project' (1994c), the remedy proposed by Habermas in the early 1980s for the side-effects of juridification.

In terms of cultural modernity, a recurrent feature of Habermas's journalism has been the critique of neoconservatism. Building on this, other conservative tendencies, which have received less attention from him, are also addressed in this study.

Chapter outlines

The following chapter is the first of four elaborating an account of social modernity in the EU. Punctuated by references to historical events, it offers a selective chronology of Habermas's political writings from the late 1970s to the era of the European Constitution. The aims are twofold. First, to demonstrate how the idea of social modernity has exerted a continual influence on Habermas's political journalism. In performing this task, the theoretical works central to this study are introduced: volumes one and two of *The Theory of Communicative Action* (TCA), *The Philosophical Discourse of Modernity* (PDM) and *Between Facts and Norms* (BFN). Juridification is argued for as the main concept behind Habermas's reflections on both the nation-state and EU. The other aim of the following chapter is to show the continuity of the reflective welfare state project as a theme of the political journalism.

In chapter 2, juridification is put forward as a metatheory of social modernity. An account of related Habermasian concepts is also set out there. The growth of the European single market is taken to parallel the earlier development of 'the bourgeois state under the absolutist regimes of Europe', a process that 'instituted the contractual rights and obligations of private persons as the condition of free enterprise in a market economy' (Ashenden, 1998: 120). Particular attention is paid to the period from the signing of the Single European Act (SEA) in 1986 to the era of the European Constitution. A preliminary engagement with theories of European integration is also undertaken, while the development of EU social policy is considered alongside sketches of institutional evolution and 'history making' agreements.

As mentioned previously, analyses of social modernity in the EU must take into account the varying relationships between member states and supranational institutions. To this end, existing approaches from the corpus of European integration theory are drawn on in chapter 3.

Thus far, discussion of the lifeworld will have focussed on its, to some extent conflictual, relationships with the market and state in the course of social evolution. An 'externalist' (Habermas, 1995: 204) view of this sort is commonly encountered in theoretical treatments of European integration, the process described, so to speak, from outside. In chapter 4, attention is given to the 'internalist' (Habermas, 1995: 204) perspective of the lifeworld, its direct experience of market and administrative imperatives. Habermas conceives of a functioning democracy as one where the lifeworld is able to resist, and even reverse, incursions by these imperatives; chapter 4 continues with an application of this democratic theory to the EU. The relationship between democracy and legitimacy it posits is relatively linear, fluctuations in one generally giving rise to variations in the other. The chapter concludes with a survey of rival accounts of democracy in the EU.

Chapter 5 commences the second part of this study, an analysis of cultural modernity at the level of the EU. Attention shifts from the *structure* of the lifeworld to the traditions that have constituted it. In the West, the Hellenic and Judeo-Christian traditions fulfilled this function; the implications of this state of affairs were examined by Max Weber. Habermas's (1997a) interpretation of Weberian concepts – disenchantment, Occidental rationalism and the Protestant ethic – is therefore central to this chapter. Having touched on the rise of science, modern art and universalism in law and moral judgement, the chapter goes on to consider the cosmopolitan conception of citizenship and identity seen by Habermas as commensurate with these cultural developments. Finally, three tendencies inimical to Habermas's conception of modernity and cosmopolitanism – those of 'Young', 'Old' and 'New' Conservatism (Habermas, 1996a) – are outlined.

Following Habermas, *combinations* of these abstract types are, in chapters 6 and 7, used to analyse actual groupings in European and American politics. Chapter 6 examines the rise in recent decades of neoconservatism. Distinctions between German and American representatives of this political family are made clear, Habermas's marginal preference for the latter explained by their orientation toward the Enlightenment. Yet it is also the American neoconservatives who are Habermas's preferred foil for postnational cosmopolitanism.

While Habermas has continued to discuss neoconservatism in recent years, he has, with the exception of some enigmatic references, neglected to monitor the successors of other conservative groupings whom he drew attention to in the early 1980s – some are considered in chapter 7. Initially, attention is given to a range of 'antiproductivist' and uniformly Eurosceptic constituencies, from the palingenetic[5] (rather than monetarist) New Right and its disciples among Eurofascist parties to sections of the antiglobalisation movement. More even than the neoconservatives, these are not categorised in terms of traditionally understood markers of left and right, but rather on the basis of their attitudes toward modernity. Productivists and enthusiasts for natural scientific explanations of human affairs – some of whom have been influenced by the aesthetic avant-garde, counterculture or other neo-Nietzschean orientations – are then approached. Among them are writers such as Michel Houellebecq,[6] J.G. Ballard and Ernst Jünger, and academics such as John Gray and Samuel Huntington. This section continues with reflection on arguably the purest *political* incarnation of this tendency to appear in the early twenty-first century: the maverick Dutch politician Pim Fortuyn, whose ascent and subsequent assassination coincided with the Constitutional Convention. The concluding section of chapter 7 shifts to

Habermas's discussion with Cardinal Joseph Ratzinger in 2004. Habermas's engagement with Catholic thought is argued for as commensurate with his earlier his championing of modernity and European integration, rather than as signifying a retreat from these processes.

Chapter 8 uses concepts derived from the accounts of social and cultural modernity to analyse empirical data collected against the background of the Constitutional Convention. The findings of interviews with Members of the European Parliament (MEPs) and institutional personnel of the radical and social democratic left are considered first. Each has at times been looked to by Habermas as a 'constituency'. Yet, as the interviews demonstrate, his conception of European integration is too idiosyncratic to have mobilised them thus far. The universalist orientations, concern with democracy and emphasis on north/south welfarist solidarity of the radical left echo Habermas's writings on the EU and Constitution. However, contra Habermas, the radical left regard positive change as possible only *in the face of* the integration process. The social democrats who were interviewed had the opposite combination of opinions. Thus, different elements of Habermas's vision of Europe appealed to the two groups without either accepting it as a whole. The chapter concludes with reflection on interviews with a variety of centrists, social partners and institutional personnel.

Notes

1 Habermas (2001c: 13).

2 This perspective contrasts with that of the late Tony Judt. Recalling the epilogue to Houellebecq's *Atomised* (1998), Judt (2005: 786) interprets the lukewarm response to Habermas and Derrida's (2003) call for reflection on Europe's identity, values and role in world affairs as evidence of the declining influence of the public intellectual. Neither the anti-Enlightenment zeitgeist that came after 9/11, nor the intellectualism of commentators, then in the ascendant, such as John Gray and Christopher Hitchens, served to qualify this view.

3 Gabriel Josipovici's work on literary modernism has considerable parallels with Habermas's account of cultural modernity.

> [Modernism] was not a "movement", like mannerism, or the name of a period. Like Romanticism, it is multifaceted and ambiguous. And it didn't begin in 1880 and end in 1930. Modernism, whenever it began, will always be with us, for it is not primarily a revolution in diction, or a response to industrialisation or the First World War, but is art coming to a consciousness of its limitations and responsibilities ...
>
> If, for the Romantics, Shakespeare and Milton were gigantic figures they could not hope to emulate, for some artists in the Renaissance their own age had already lost contact with authority. Albrecht Dürer sums this up in his two parallel engravings of 1514 *Saint Jerome in His Study* and *Melencolia I*. The former shows us the saint who gave the Latin west its Bible, at ease with tradition, working away peacefully in his room. The latter shows us a figure many modern artists have identified with: a wild-eyed, impotent giantess in a bleak landscape, surrounded by instruments of making, but incapable of making anything because she is unable to

connect with any tradition. Rabelais, Cervantes and Sterne later explored this predicament in comic style and, for that reason, they seem to us to be strikingly modern, the true contemporaries of Borges and Beckett. (Josipovici, 2010: 2)

4   Habermas's writings, it is worth noting, prescribe some form of statehood as a terminus for the European project: an article on the Irish rejection of the Lisbon Treaty, for example, reiterated the need for a 'cautious harmonization of tax and economic policy, and the gradual assimilation of social security systems within the EU' (Habermas, 2008a: 2). Drawing on the *Sozialstaat* concepts of TCA and BFN, neither Eriksen and Fossum (2000) nor the author depart significantly from such views.

The elaboration of alternate 'futures' for the EU has been taken up by other established scholars. As well as Schmitter, whose work on the subject included the formulation of two influential concepts: *consortio* and *condominio* (1998b: 136), McCormick (2007: 22n36, 235n13) cites the 'very different' approaches of Bellamy and Castiglione, Joerges and Neyer, and Scharpf, alongside his own, as exemplary of this grouping.

Nevertheless, in terms of institutional structure these scholars do not diverge significantly from the siege model of the EU that features in this study. Where they do differ from it, however, is their belief in a segmentation of Europe's *public sphere* comparable with that of its administration. Thus, while deliberation might thrive *within* the 'micro-policy-making publics' of the comitology system (McCormick, 2007: 20), for example, discrete contexts such as these are not encompassed by a continental public sphere linked closely with the European Parliament. McCormick describes this outlook as 'incompletely Habermasian to the extent that it ... (1) dismisses or at the very least downgrades the participation or "say" of those *less* affected but still concretely affected by a policy; (2) virtually abandons participation of or sanctioning by the polity at large through either constitutional or statutory law' (McCormick, 2007: 23).

5   In fascist studies, the term *palingenetic* denotes the centrality to an ideology of a myth of national rebirth or renewal (Griffin, 1993: 2).

6   For an early, albeit disparaging, social-theoretic engagement with Houellebecq's writing, see Axel Honneth's Tanner Lecture on the concept of reification (2005: 93).

PART I

Social modernity

1

Habermas on European integration

This chapter addresses two features of Habermas's oeuvre. These form the basis for the account of social modernity that follows in chapters 2 to 4. First, there is the influence that the concept of juridification has had on Habermas's journalistic writings. Though most evident in his reflections on the nation-state, juridification also informed Habermas's (2001a, 2005) calls for constitutional deliberation. Reading his work in this way diverges from the more usual separation of its academic and journalistic aspects; it is the latter practice that Habermas, following Max Weber, has himself encouraged (Outhwaite, 1996: 5, 371). Habermas's account (1996a, 1997a, 1998a) of the differentiation of knowledge into value spheres – those of science and knowledge, morality and law, and art and art criticism – also encourages a distinction of this kind; it was, after all, a defence of conceptual boundaries that prompted his well-known critique of poststructuralism (Habermas, 1998a). The case for a separation between bodies of work has perhaps been enforced further by the audiences to which they appeal: those familiar with the journalism, which often appears in the form of newspaper articles, may have only a passing acquaintance with the academic writing. The second feature of Habermas's work examined here is the continuity *within* his journalism of the reflective welfare state project.

Historical events and Habermas's scholarly writings provide a background context for the journalism survey that follows. Original, German, publication dates are used in order to situate each text accurately in time. The survey is divided into two parts. The first examines the critical and cautious attitude toward European integration exhibited by Habermas from the early 1960s. The increasingly positive attitude he has shown since the early 1990s is then considered.

However, such a neat periodisation should not obscure the continuity and recurrence of themes. Habermas's 'Eurosceptic'[1] phase actually coincided with a gradual rejection of the nation-state, separable into three stages. The first stage, running up to the early 1980s, saw him (Habermas, 1986a: 85) rejecting the European project out of hand. With the second, spanning the early to mid 1980s, he began to lose faith in the capacity for complex socio-economic problems to be solved within the purview of the nation-state, while retaining a critical attitude toward the European project (Habermas, 1986b, 1998b: 366–7). The third stage, coinciding with his 'legal turn', began in the mid to late 1980s – though retaining an emphasis on the Federal Republic of Germany (FRG), Habermas now introduced the idea of 'constitutional patriotism', a key component of his later vision for Europe (Habermas, 1994b: 256). What of his 'Europhile' phase? An initially cautious (Habermas, 1992a) stance took a decade to flower into outright enthusiasm (Habermas, 2001a, 2005).

Another commonly made distinction contrasts Habermas's earlier radical-democratic orientation with the legal-democratic one of his later work. On closer analysis, this too is brought into question. First, because Habermas (1986b: 67) had long ago rejected the idea, once common on the non-Leninist left, of a democratic 'transformation of the capitalist economy according to models of self-management and council-based administration'. And second, because his support for the Constitution placed him at the utopian fringe of the social democratic intellectuals and politicians constituting his peer group.

Postwar scepticism

While taking inspiration from Kant, Hegel, Marx and Rawls, among others, Habermas has tried to move beyond their subject-centred modes of thought. In place of the latter, he has favoured an intersubjective approach that stresses communication *between* subjects. This has been a feature of his work since the early 1960s. Initially, it was given empirical expression in *The Structural Transformation of the Public Sphere* (1962). A theoretical treatment followed in the Gauss Lectures of 1971 (Habermas, 2001b).

The Structural Transformation of the Public Sphere takes the bourgeois 'public sphere' as its object of analysis. The development of this social formation, a set of interlinked fora for the open discussion of contemporary affairs and state policy among 'informed outsiders', is charted from the coffee houses and salons of eighteenth-century Europe to its twentieth-century decline in the face of organised interests concerned to modulate public opinion. Conceived of as a 'higher level' intersubjectivity (Habermas, 1994c: 67, 1998a: 359) than that of everyday discourse, the public sphere is the cornerstone of Habermas's writings.

The Gauss Lectures saw a move from the 'philosophy of consciousness' to the 'philosophy of communication'. The former concerns the subject-centred conception of cognition and rationality characteristic of early modern thought. The philosophy of communication encompasses intersubjective approaches, such as Habermas's own, relevant to the networked, media-saturated conditions of late modernity.

In 'Conservatism and capitalist crisis', written in 1978, Habermas looked to contemporary concerns (1986b). The article examined the challenges to the welfare state posed by advanced capitalism at the time of the energy crisis. It also touched on the radical political currents of the period, to which Habermas would return throughout the 1980s. Written just prior to Margaret Thatcher's and Ronald Reagan's election victories, the article displayed considerable prescience in relation to the monetarist New Right. In terms of New Social Movements (NSMs), Habermas placed particular hope in feminism, due to its fidelity to the universalist aspirations of previous bourgeois emancipation movements. The Greens, on the other hand, were identified with a more varied, even antimodern, set of views. Their choice, Habermas later argued, was whether to mount a critique of productivism comparable with those of romantic social movements of the early industrial era or to develop a pragmatic approach. Tension between the two orientations has characterised the history of the German Green party, though the leadership of Joshcka Fischer shifted the balance in favour of its *Realo* wing. This tension has also been a theme of Habermas's social theory, which makes the distinction between *traditional* ways of life, whose disruption is viewed by him as acceptable, if traumatic, and those *post-traditional* alternatives that are themselves the fruits of modernity. The cultivation and protection of the latter has been among the roles attributed by him to NSMs.

'Conservatism and capitalist crisis' reflected Habermas's concern with a 'modernisation' of Marxist theory. This effort had spanned the 1970s, with the publication of *Legitimation Crisis* in 1973 and TCA in 1981. The former considered classical Marxism's base-superstructure model, and the accounts of capitalist crisis associated with it. In their place was offered a conception of advanced capitalism that showed how crisis phenomena could be displaced onto non-economic spheres of life, 'giving rise to more diffuse crises of legitimation and motivation' (Outhwaite, 1996: 17). The varieties of cultural and psychological pathology caused by incursions into the lifeworld of market and administrative imperatives would be explored at length in TCA.

A remark in 'Political experience and the renewal of Marxist theory', first published in 1979, encapsulated Habermas's early scepticism toward the European project. Yet there was also a note of ambivalence, a hope for the gradual attenuation of nationalism: 'I've never been a fan of the idea of a "unified Europe", even when it was fashionable, and I'm still not one today. But one does have to be glad to see a certain growing integration of the European nations' (Habermas, 1986a: 85).

The first half of the 1980s would see the publication of two of Habermas's major works, prior to his explorations of democracy and law in the late eighties and early nineties. These were, of course, TCA (volumes I and II), published in 1981, and PDM, which followed in 1985. PDM showed how continental thought since Hegel had either remained with the philosophy of the subject, and the account of reason tied to it, or, a trajectory beginning with Nietzsche, rejected subject-centred rationality entirely. Only by embracing an intersubjective perspective, it was argued, could the aporia of the subject be overcome without an abandonment of reason. The appearance of TCA and PDM coincided with a rightward shift in German politics, the election of Helmut Kohl in 1982 inaugurating sixteen years of Christian Democratic government. As previously, it was in Habermas's journalism that theoretical concerns were made relevant to contemporary affairs.

'Conservative politics, work, socialism and Utopia today' (Habermas, 1986d), an article from 1984, continued to chart the fortunes of the welfare state. Yet along with the rise of the New Right, Habermas argued that this bureaucratic structure was threatened by its inability to solve by mere financial means the increasingly subtle ways in which economic and administrative systems, including the welfare state itself, were affecting the lives of its clients. Such deformations of the lifeworld could, he suggested, be better diagnosed and resisted by NSMs such as the Greens. The welfare state's limitations stemmed from the productivist ethos underpinning it, a belief that production and labour are the primary forces shaping social life, and that it is exclusively in terms of compensation for lost work that individuals can be protected from the side-effects of the market and administrative systems.

Ideas from TCA continued to surface in *The New Conservatism* (1985), yet this selection of political essays also hinted at the legal-democratic turn that Habermas's thought would take as the 1980s drew to a close. The call for a more reflective version of the welfare state project was again heard. This required NSMs and the public sphere to act on the welfare state administration in much the same way as the latter had 'domesticated' the market. It would be futile to create a further bureaucratic authority to 'police' the welfare state from the outside: this would simply intensify lifeworld colonisation. The only option was continually to 'police the boundary' between the subsystems of market and state, on the one hand, and the lives of citizens, on the other. An intersubjective public sphere capable of resisting system complexity in this way constituted for Habermas the final decoupling of 'utopian' aspirations from the productivist paradigm, their traditional basis among movements of the left. Sociological research seemed at the time to encourage this move beyond productivism. In a speech given to the Spanish parliament in 1984, Habermas (1994c: 53–60) drew on Claus Offe's argument to the effect that work was now less of an influence on the evolution of society than had previously been the case.

PDM featured a questioning of the nation-state, though not, as yet, the suggestion of an alternative. The nation-state had proved uniquely capable of balancing universalist principles with the particularisms of the cultures in which they had arisen, while other institutions – the Communist Party, North Atlantic Treaty Organisation (NATO), European Community (EC), etc. – had not (Habermas, 1998a: 366–7). In the absence of a viable alternative to the nation-state, a network of deracinated market and administrative systems might take over the task of governance, a future intimated by the continental economies of the EC and USA. Only Europe's modernist and Enlightenment traditions – as yet lacking an institutional vehicle for their realisation – offered alternatives to the social Darwinism of the latter.

With the 'Law and morality' lectures delivered in 1986, Habermas embarked on an avenue of research that would culminate with the publication of BFN in 1992. Of particular importance was his use, in 1987, of Dolf Sternberger's term 'constitutional patriotism' (Habermas, 1994d: 256). This would become synonymous with Habermas's legal-democratic theory in the years to come. It encapsulated his belief that constitutional frameworks, legitimised by public deliberation, can to some extent 'induce' the sort of political identification and belonging sought through the reflective welfare state project. Hence, this shift in Habermas's thought ought not to be seen as an abandonment of civil society in favour positive law. Indeed, alongside the novelist Günter Grass, Habermas (1994a) had criticised the German reunification process for relying excessively on the latter, pointing to the 'normative deficit' that came from its realisation through market and administrative forms of integration.

From Maastricht to Lisbon

'What does socialism mean today?', written in 1990, returned to one of Habermas's main themes: the redundancy of traditional Marxist approaches emphasising class conflict and the labour theory of value (Habermas, 1990a). Yet the essay also stated that it would never now be possible to know whether a reform of state socialism might have been achievable from within. Declining to rule out this alternative path of modernity, the *possibility* of democratic socialism was implicitly retained, again upsetting a neat division of Habermas's work into radical and legal-democratic phases. Now, however, only by achieving the right *balance* between power, money and solidarity was it thought that something approaching 'socialism' might arise in complex societies.

Despite the fall of the Berlin Wall, Habermas remained relatively silent toward the European project. Nevertheless, he had begun to concede that social democratic ends had been possible at the level of the nation-state only until the end of the 1980s (Habermas, 1998c).

With 'Citizenship and national identity: some reflections on the future of Europe' an affirmative attitude toward postnational politics began gradually to emerge, informed, no doubt, by the debate on the Maastricht Treaty that was going on at the time; the outmanoeuvring of Margaret Thatcher by François Mitterrand and Helmut Kohl during the Maastricht negotiations (Kaiser, 2007: 324) could not have escaped Habermas's attention, particularly given his concern at the rise of the New Right. However, he conceded that the constitutional patriotism of a 'future Federal Republic of Europe' would have to be anchored in the particularism of its constituent nations, and he asked whether a 'parliamentarisation of the Brussels expertocracy' would be enough to democratically influence an administrative process that had increasingly taken on purely economic criteria of rationality (1992a: 9).

In the course of an interview conducted in 1993, Habermas suggested that opposition to a 'system driven' integration process might one day change into calls for more democracy at the level of the EU. Yet debate on a constitution was not yet described explicitly as a catalyst to democratisation, nor, indeed, to the rise of a continental public sphere. Habermas claimed that intellectuals talked 'about Europe without ever doing anything for it' (Carleheden and Gabriëls, 1996: 16), adding them to the radical and social democratic left as potential agents of a postnational politics. This intellectual call to arms anticipated an account he would later give of the formation of the German state: 'it was writers and historians, and scholars and intellectuals in general who laid the groundwork for ... Bismarck's subsequent diplomatic and military unification of the state by propagating the more or less imaginary unity of the "cultural nation"' (Habermas, 1998f: 397).

As well as exhibiting a more favourable view of law, the interview previewed another feature of BFN. Resistance to market and administrative imperatives by the public sphere was described as a 'siege model' of democracy; yet Habermas suggested that an alternate model could institute a 'more comprehensive process of democratisation'. This sluice-gate model was described as a 'constitutionally based political system consist[ing] of a centre and a periphery [where in] ... order that citizens may influence the centre, that is parliament, courts and administration, the communication flows arising in the periphery have to pass through the sluice-gate of democratic and constitutional procedures' (Carleheden and Gabriëls, 1996: 3–4). With this second model, then, Habermas broached the possibility of democratically modulating, rather than just containing, the administrative system.

'Beyond the nation-state?', a lecture given in 1997 (see Habermas, 2000), focussed on political economy and international affairs, particularly the weakness of states in the face of the global market. With the end of the 'golden age' of the welfare state, Habermas foresaw the 'return of a problem as old as capitalism itself', one that had to a certain degree been solved in the postwar era: '[h]ow to exploit the allocative and discovering functions of self-regulating markets effectively without having to accept unequal distribution and social costs which are at variance with the preconditions for an integration of liberal societies?'. Habermas considered the strategies put forward in the UK by the governing Labour Party. These were oriented toward improving national competitiveness by increasing the flexibility of the labour market, and by increasing training and research and development. Yet such approaches, Habermas suggested, would only be beneficial to the poor and unemployed if the jobs so created were subsidised through, for example, negative income tax schemes. However, it was a more radical version of this strategy that appealed to him at the time, connecting his vision for the EU with his prescriptions of the early 1980s for reform of the welfare state. A guaranteed minimum income, suggested initially by Gorz and subsequently by Offe, would finally act to sever the link between income and employment. The 'economic society', with the full-time wage earner at its centre, would thereby be brought to an end (Habermas, 2000: 29–33; Gorz, 1981).

The lecture also brought Habermas's theoretical discussions with Niklas Luhmann to bear on questions of postnational politics. Habermas distinguished between the Luhmannian use of the term 'reflexive', exemplified by the workings of a market economy, and his own 'self-reflective' position, delineated in terms of the public sphere (Habermas, 2000: 39). Habermas understood the 'Third Way' politics of the British Labour Party as conducive to a Luhmannian future for the EU, with market and administrative systems given free-reign to modulate the public sphere.

The Postnational Constellation, a collection of essays first published in 1998, brought together a wide variety of themes. An overview of the twentieth-century charted the transformation of the human 'masses' (whether classes, nations, armies or political organisations) into the networks and 'scattered monads' of the suceeding epoch (2001c: 57–80). Other themes included Europe's growing underclass, and the fact that, with developments in information technology, the mastery of *territory* had given way to the mastery of *speed* as the guiding principle of international affairs.[2]

In the absence of a postnational politics, it was again argued, states would increasingly be at the mercy of the global market (2001c: 81–144). Habermas drew on Karl Polanyi's *The Great Transformation* (1944) in diagnosing the situation faced by the EU. The growth of international trade in the nineteenth-century had, according to Polanyi, culminated in social and economic collapse, leading ultimately to fascism. Yet the Bretton Woods system had subsequently provided the basis for the welfare state compromise widely adopted in the developed world (2001c: 11).

Themes from PNC were pursued further in the following year. 'The European nation state and the pressures of globalisation' (1999a) depicted Mitterrand's failed economic programme of the early 1980s as an indication of the waning of state power in relation to the global market. Yet Habermas declined in the article to elaborate on Mitterrand and Delors' engagement with Europe, a postnational shift that grew from similar concerns to his own. Delors had, as European Commission president, promoted what he called the European Social Model (ESM). Habermas's reluctance to identify with Delors' project was most likely due to its productivism, and perhaps also to its debt to Catholic thought (Ross, 1995: 16–17).

In 'A constitution for Europe?', Habermas (2001a) recommended bicameral federalism as a political structure for the EU. This he championed against a looser arrangement espoused by Siedentop (2000), who doubted that mass publics could be mobilised behind an ambitious federalist goal. Habermas thought that Siedentop had missed the point of the European endeavour. For while it was true that the EU's constitutional debate lacked the novelty of the one conducted in Philadelphia by the Founding Fathers or that of the delegates to the Assemblée Nationale in Paris, Europeans were nevertheless faced with an urgent task: that of *preserving* the democratic and welfarist achievements of the nation-state 'beyond its own limits'. Integral to this would be the incorporation of the Charter of Fundamental Rights into the Constitution (Habermas, 2001a: 5–6). The article continued by elaborating an 'offensive' version of Third Way politics, against the 'defensive' varieties of Anthony Giddens, Gerhard Schröeder and Tony Blair. Fiscal harmonisation was also called for, with praise for Lionel Jospin's efforts in this direction (Habermas, 2001a: 26).

Of particular importance, Habermas argued, was mass deliberation on the contents of the Constitution. This, it was hoped, would effect an opening and interpenetration of national public spheres. Habermas's attitude contrasted with the cautious, even pessimistic, ones of other pro-Europeans. No doubt this was due to the theory underpinning it, in light of which continental deliberation could act as a bridge between the siege and sluice gate models of democracy. In a series of articles written after 9/11 (Habermas, 2003a; Habermas and Derrida, 2003), however, Habermas depicted mobilisations closer to the siege model of TCA. His discussion of the mass protests against Western intervention in Iraq saw a shift from law and professional politicians to intellectuals and civil society as the architects of a European consciousness. Indeed, it was at this time that Habermas placed his name alongside that of French philosopher Jacques Derrida – toward whose writings he had previously directed a critical gaze – in calling for a common European foreign policy (Habermas, 2003a; Habermas and Derrida, 2003).

In an article for the *Nouvel Observateur*, Habermas (2005) addressed the French public on the subject of the constitution, lending his support to the 'Yes' campaign in its closing stages. Adopting a more combative and partisan stance – 'social democratic – in the largest sense of the term' (2005: 3) – than previously, he rehearsed a number of his main themes. Striking a topical note, he also encouraged the equation of opposition to American intervention in Iraq with support for the Constitution:[3]

> [George] Bush is the one who would rejoice at the failure of the European constitution, for it would allow Europe to develop a common foreign and security policy with enough soft power to bolster opposition to the neoconservative view of global order. (Habermas, 2005: 4)

Constitutional deliberation might even have an impact on the zeitgeist, which Habermas had thought of since the 1970s as characterised by 'cultural pessimism' (McCarthy, 1997: vii). The goal was to take the project of modernity further forward. The 'prolonged depression' in Europe anticipated by Habermas (2005: 4) in the event of a French 'No' vote would form part of a deeper civilisation malaise, not just be a recurrence of Europessimism.

Even after the rejection of the Lisbon Treaty by Irish voters in 2008, Habermas (2008a) continued to campaign for the legitimation of Europe's constitutional order. In an article from the same year, he remembered the role played by Wolfgang Abendroth, his habilitation supervisor, in the political and intellectual life of postwar Germany (Habermas, 2008b). Abendroth's contribution, he suggested, bore comparison with that of Hermann Heller, a constitutionalist of the Weimar era whose 'defence of social democracy resonates famously in the commitments of Germany's Basic Law' (Joerges and Castiglione, 2005: 13–14). Continuities between Habermas and Heller can also be discerned. As Joerges notes, 'Heller was probably the first to deliver a systematic constitutional theory in which the social and the rule of law were synthesised' (Joerges and Castiglione, 2005: 13). In doing so, he anticipated not only Habermas's emphasis on social rights as a prerequisite of a meaningful democracy (Heller, 2002: 260–2), but also his insistence that legal principles do not 'come from outside of our general social practices', and, thus, that it 'is a condition of any modern attempt to justify the state or law that its justification be immanent' (Dyzenhaus, 2002: 252). Asserting, against the tenor of the times, that only through the deliberation of its publics might Europe's constitution be legitimated, Habermas held to the democratic rigours of this heritage.

Notes

1 Euroscepticism was not uncommon among the left in the postwar era. The following piece by Alasdair MacIntyre is therefore noteworthy, preceding Habermas's interest in the EU by just over a quarter of a century:

> The British Left is unhappy about foreigners, partly because they theorise. The weakness of its complacent pragmatism is doubly revealed when it is confronted simultaneously with questions of theory and questions about foreigners at one and the same time, as it is over the Common Market. So with a few slick references to Gallipoli and Vimy Ridge, the Labour Party constitutes itself as the party of the English-Speaking Empire, and all through the balancing of pros and cons nobody pointed out that 'Socialism in One Country' is a sad slogan for a Gaitskell to inherit from a Stalin.
>
> What criterion should a socialist use here? It belongs both to the ends and to the means of socialism that it is international. One end is a new mass democracy in which economic and political institutions serve rather than master people; but no revolutionary changes of this kind can be insulated from the outside world. Either, as Lenin saw, they expand to an international scale, or they regress. And the labour movement which brings about such changes will have to be genuinely internationalised, breaking through the narrow bureaucratised national forms of the present-day labour movement. The last intention of the fathers of nineteenth-century capitalism was to lay the foundations of the labour movement; but they did. The last intention of the founders of the Common Market is to pave the way

for a United Socialist States of Europe. But I am all for taking them by the hand as a preliminary to taking them by ... but that would be tactless.

I do not understand those socialists who are against Franco-German capitalism, but somehow prefer British capitalism. I detest the anti-German chauvinism of the anti-Common Marketeers. I can see nothing but good in an enforced dialogue with the exciting movements on the Italian Left. Labour leaders should be using the demand for equalisation upwards of welfare benefits in the Treaty of Rome to dramatise the conservative dreariness of our (false) national belief that Britain leads in welfare. CND-ers should be considering internationalised non-violent action against nuclear crimes. We should all be posing the problems of socialism as they would be, rescued from the dead clichés of our national stereotypes. But that would drive us all into socialist theory. We should have to take seriously brands of European Marxists and brands of European anti-Marxists of whom we had scarcely heard. How much nicer to use the Common Market as the one scapegoat in whom Gaitskell and Cousins and Foot and Jay can all agree to bury their hatchet. But when the scapegoat gets up and walks away, what will they do with their hatchets to each other then? (MacIntyre, 1963: 65)

2   See also Paul Virilio's *Speed and Politics* (1977).
3   Two articles in the *Financial Times* echoed Habermas's belief that sentiment critical of President Bush might be harnessed to the cause of the Constitution. Late in 2004, Wolfgang Münchau argued that 'Mr Bush's re-election ... should, for example, make it easier for pro-European politicians to sell to voters the as yet unratified constitutional treaty' (Münchau, 2004). A month later, Quentin Peel made a comparable case: 'another unlikely group is lining up to take sides with European eurosceptics: American conservatives and neo-conservatives ... Many who believe [Tony Blair] ... did the right thing by backing Mr Bush in Iraq think the EU constitution would stop him doing the same again. The same analysis might well persuade those who opposed the Iraq war to vote for the constitution' (Peel, 2004b).

2

Metatheory

As the journalism survey of the previous chapter showed, Habermas views the EU as repeating the process of juridification beyond the nation-state, initially in terms of the single market, and then, gradually, in its civil, political and social dimensions. Yet he also acknowledges major differences between this continental cycle of juridification and the centuries of development that culminated in the welfare state. Juridification can be thought of as a metatheory of social modernity, a statement of its ontological assumptions.

Habermas's account of social evolution is considered in the following section. This describes primitive and traditional stages of development, and the subsequent onset of juridification. Section two then looks in greater detail at the concepts of 'system' and 'lifeworld' so central to Habermas's thought; he conceives of the EU as an *intensification* of juridification, rather than as a qualitative shift from law to an alternative mechanism of social evolution, such as information technology.

Subsequent sections extrapolate the concept of juridification to the level of the EU. Five attributes specific to EU juridification are identified. Successive historical trajectories of continental juridification are then delineated. These are categorised in terms of the 'neo-Latin' ideal types developed by Schmitter (1998b: 133–6), rather than Westphalian or imperial models drawn from elsewhere;[1] in Schimtter's terminology, post-Maastricht juridification is found to correspond with the trajectory of *condominio*. Integration theories such as neofunctionalism are considered in historical context in these closing sections, as is EU social policy.

Social evolution

TCA sets out a three-stage account of social evolution. The first stage refers to tribal societies of the sorts studied in Africa, Southeast Asia and Australia by English anthropologists of the early twentieth century. The lifeworld and market-administrative system of a tribe can be thought of as coextensive. Traditional societies, organised around a state, come next. Finally, modern societies have seen both elements of the market-administrative system differentiated out, often beyond the influence of the lifeworld (Habermas, 1995: 153–6); it is in relation to modern societies that juridification is spoken of.

Analysis of a tribe can be carried out exclusively from the system or lifeworld perspective because market and administrative functions are structured and conceptualised entirely in terms of the traditions of which the lifeworld is composed. Indeed, linguistically mediated communication constitutes social structures, resulting in a high degree of congruence between institutions, persons and worldviews (Habermas, 1995: 156). In place of state coercion, the power of sanction is drawn from sacred norms. The combination of kinship structures and mythical structures of consciousness means that tribal societies can approximate to the ideal of a 'total institution', defining members' roles and the boundary of the social unit as a whole. Increases in complexity, and hence structure, are still possible, however. First, a tribe can become more complex by internal differentiation through marriage – the multiplication of family groups is compared with the internal segmentation of a cell as depicted in the biological sciences. Second, complexity can increase through different tribes coming together into larger structures. In both cases, the exchange of women through the rules of marriage results simultaneously in lifeworld and system integration (Habermas, 1995: 158–63). As throughout social evolution, such increases in complexity can only be stabilised through the introduction of new principles of organisation. In the case of the simplest *egalitarian* tribal societies, seniority and male gender combine to denote which members of the tribe will take on the role of coordinating its affairs. Further levels of complexity give rise to *hierarchical* tribal societies, where familial status and descent provide stratifications of rank. Hence, both egalitarian and hierarchical tribal societies are segmentally differentiated through *exchange* relations, and stratified through *power* relations. The two means of differentiation recur in the course of social evolution, ultimately in the forms of the capitalist market and state apparatus (Habermas, 1995: 164–72).

With the development of 'genuinely political power' that no longer derived its authenticity from dominant descent groups, but rather from judicial means of sanction, authority became detached from kinship structures. Organisational complexity now required an administrative apparatus both independent and encompassing of the lifeworld. As the empires of antiquity showed, such societies could sustain far greater, indeed *civilisational*, levels of complexity than the most developed of tribes. Thus, social stratification came to be manifested in the form of hierarchical class societies (Habermas, 1995: 165). These had a lifespan second only to their tribal predecessors, for Habermas writes of them with reference to both the empires of antiquity and the European feudal system that preceded the modern state. Traditional societies also saw the development of markets steered by the symbolically generalised exchange relations of money. Unlike the modern case, however, the market was yet to alter the fabric of everyday life. This would only happen at the close of the European middle-ages, when the economy began to detach itself from the political order (Habermas, 1995: 165), and the roles of wage earner and taxpayer came to constitute identities and forms of life in themselves.

System and lifeworld

The lifeworld is thought of by Habermas as 'a reservoir of taken-for-granteds, of unshaken convictions that participants in communication draw upon in cooperative processes of interpretation' (Habermas, 1995: 124). The system comprises integrated networks of institutional, legal and market organisation. Habermas sees

> social evolution as a second order process of differentiation: system and lifeworld are differentiated in the sense that the complexity of the one and the rationality of the other grow. But it is not only qua system and qua lifeworld that they are differentiated; they get differentiated from one another at the same time ... [This] uncoupling of system and lifeworld is depicted in such a way that the lifeworld, which is at first coextensive with a scarcely differentiated social system, gets cut down more and more to one subsystem among others. In the process, system mechanisms get further and further detached from the social structures through which social integration takes place ... [Modern] societies attain a level of system differentiation at which increasingly autonomous organisations are connected to one another via delinguistified media of communication: these systemic mechanisms ... steer social intercourse that has been largely disconnected from norms and values. (Habermas, 1995: 153–4)

Market and administrative systems utilise the specialised 'languages' of price and law, while the lifeworld rests on the practice of everyday speech, sharing the latter's *telos* toward mutual understanding. That the lifeworld must resist unwarranted incursions by systemic imperatives, lest these become the sole rationales of social life, is the core of Habermas's democratic theory (1995, 1998b).

Kinship relations and stratification of rank and political office were the means by which tribes and premodern states respectively anchored successive levels of systemic differentiation; in modern states, this role has been performed by law (Habermas, 1995: 165–8). What of the EU? As stated previously, European integration constitutes, from a Habermasian perspective, an intensification of juridification rather than a shift to a new stage of social organisation; though facilitated by, for example, information technology, the integration process is unthinkable without law. Ashenden summarises:

> The first stage of this process of juridification began with the establishment of the bourgeois state under the absolutist regimes of Europe. This regulated sovereign monopoly over coercion and instituted the contractual rights and obligations of

private persons as the condition for free enterprise in a market economy. The second stage, the bourgeois constitutional state, regulated individual rights to life, liberty and property against the political authority of the monarch. The third stage, the creation of the democratic constitutional state in the wake of the French Revolution, brought political emancipation. The fourth stage of juridification, that of the twentieth-century democratic welfare state, secured freedoms and social rights against the state. (Ashenden, 1998: 120)

Five attributes of EU juridification

Rereading TCA through the lens of Habermas's later journalistic writings, it is possible to discern five attributes specific to EU juridification. First, juridification beyond the nation-state suggests the EU as the primary 'level-of-analysis' (Singer, 1961) for investigations of European affairs, though domestic and global factors remain highly significant. Indeed, the continuing importance of member states to juridification, and their being the site of democratic legitimacy for the European project as a whole, is acknowledged by Habermas (2001a: 22) in his call for a 'European Union of Nation-States'.

The account of juridification put forward in TCA covers a considerable time-span, progressing from the era of monarchical absolutism to that of the welfare state. Hence, a second sense in which EU juridification differs from the precedent set by its member states is simply the 'speed' of its occurrence since the 1950s (Habermas, 2001c: 48–57).

Perhaps a consequence of this pace, a third feature of EU juridification has been the 'complexity' of the market-administration that has arisen from it. For Habermas (1995), systemic complexity already characterised mature welfare state democracies. In the case of the EU as a whole, however, it is exacerbated by the widely varying integrative logics of disparate policy areas, certainly in contrast to the comparatively centripetal precedent of the nation-state (Grewal, 2005: 195).

Being shaped by globalisation is the fourth respect in which EU juridification diverges from the historical example of the nation-state. Prominent among the features of globalisation is the contribution made by information technology to the growth of market and administrative networks (Habermas, 2001c: 48–57). Castells' empirical survey of globalisation confirms this, linking information technology intimately with economic integration as a defining feature of the European project (Castells, 1999: 339–50).

Finally, the juridification of the EU has arguably served and been shaped by the creation of a single market to a greater extent than was the case with the nation-state (Habermas, 2005: 2). Civil, political and social legislation originating with the EU has arguably had more to do with anchoring it in the lifeworld than providing a buffer of citizens' rights against its market-administrative imperatives (Streeck and Schmitter, 1991; Leibfried, 2005: 274–5).

Trajectories of continental juridification

Given its novelty, how might the current trajectory of EU juridification be represented? Comparisons can be made between the EU and previous social formations (Zielonka, 2000), yet this approach tends toward surface description, rather than exposing the underlying logics of the polities under consideration. Perhaps for this reason, Schmitter's (1998b) work has had considerable influence, its insightfulness a function of abstraction. In relation to this study, Schmitter's effort at categorisation is also valuable in offering several permutations of market-administrative integration (of which the territorial nation-state is but a single example), all of which are compatible with the thesis of continental juridification.

Schmitter's main claim

> is that all forms of modern politics are rooted in representation ... rulers and ruled have relied increasingly on regularised mechanisms of indirect participation to communicate with each other. *Grosso modo*, these linkages conform to two different principles of aggregation: the *territorial* and the *functional*. It is the mix of territorial and functional constituencies, along with their corresponding relations of authority and accountability, that defines the type of polity. (Schmitter, 1998b: 134)

Four market-administrative categories stem from this schema: 1. *stato* (fixed functional and fixed territorial constituencies); 2. *confederatio* (fixed functional and variable territorial constituencies); 3. *consortio* (variable functional and fixed territorial constituencies); and 4. *condominio* (variable functional and variable territorial constituencies). Viewed historically, juridification in postwar Europe has corresponded with each of these categories in turn.

1. Initially, the European project seemed set on the juridification trajectory of *stato*.

> The territorial boundaries of ... authority would be fixed definitively and surround a physically contiguous space. Membership would be irreversible ... [although national] and subnational units might not disappear – especially in the federalist versions of this outcome ... On the functional side, there would be a fixed allocation of competencies among a variety of separate agencies operating within a cumulative division of labour – normally coordinated through a common budgeting process. (Schmitter, 1998b: 135)

The neofunctionalism of Haas and his contemporaries predicted something of this sort. Indeed, there seemed in the early years of European integration to be numerous instances of 'spillover', a cornerstone of the neofunctionalist approach, the idea that 'a given action, related to a specific goal, creates a situation in which the original goal can be assured only by taking further actions' (Hix, 1994: 5). As Cram notes:

Not only had the Rome Treaties been signed in 1957, providing a good example of *sectoral spill-over*, but, by the early 1960s, a number of members of the European Free Trade Association (EFTA) had begun to apply for membership of the EEC. Hence a type of *geographical spill-over* had also begun. *Political spill-over*, was in clear evidence, as interest groups mobilised around the issue of the Common Agricultural Policy. (Cram, 1998: 47–8)

What of European social policy? After an initial phase of 'benign neglect', Commission activism seemed to indicate a neofunctionalist dynamic there as well. From the early 1960s, the Commission pressed member states to fulfil treaty obligations in the area, attempted to expand its own competences through maximalist interpretations of the Treaty of Rome, sought to foster European corporatism and, in line with the labour mobility requirements of the Common Market, pushed for the harmonisation of social security systems; Commission rhetoric suggested a comprehensive federalisation of welfare in the future (Cram, 1997). Nevertheless, Cram notes how the

> Commission's early high-profile support for the social dimension may have been less a sign of its commitment to social progress than a means by which it sought to expand its competence in this field. When it became clear that the member states were unwilling to support a broad interpretation of the Commission's activities in the social field, but would continue to issue ambiguous statements of support for the social dimension, the Commission sought to justify the extension of its activities by emphasising the social aspects of economic integration. (Cram, 1997: 35)

2. The second trajectory of continental juridification anticipated features of Schmitter's *confederatio.* The latter is described as

> a more loosely coupled arrangement in which the identity and role of territorial units would be allowed to vary, while the distribution of functional constituencies and competencies would be rigorously fixed and separated in order to protect members from encroachment by central authorities ... Members would retain their autonomy and be relatively free to enter and exit. Each could negotiate its own differentiated relation to the unit as a whole, but, once a member, would be strictly bound to contribute to the few, cumulative and coincident functions devolved upon central institutions, e.g. common currency, liberalisation of trade flows, environmental protection. (Schmitter, 1998b: 133–6)

Confederatio brings to mind the practice and theory of intergovernmentalism, which places emphasis on the actions of individual states and views integration as a 'zero-sum-game', where in the case of vital issues 'losses are not compensated by gains on other issues' (Hix, 1994: 6). The heyday of the intergovernmentalist perspective saw a hiatus in neofunctionalist theorising, and the process of spillover at its centre.

> Within a few short years De Gaulle had vetoed the UK membership application (hence curtailing the process of geographical spill-over), the French 'empty chair

policy' of 1965 had put paid, at least in the short term, to any notion of Commission activism and its encouragement of political spill-over, and, finally, the oil crisis and recession of the early 1970s had brought even the automaticity of sectoral spill-over into question. (Cram, 1998: 48)

The term 'Europessimism' is commonly applied to this period. However, incremental steps forward continued to be made. Mazey notes how the development of the European Parliament's (EP) budgetary powers in 1970 and 1975 gave it increased leverage over the Council of Ministers; this would provide it with new opportunities to seek allies among the member states in support of its ongoing campaign for increased legislative powers (Mazey, 1996: 32–3). Similarly, it has been suggested, attention to the role of the European Court of Justice (ECJ) as an agent of the integration process is necessary for a more balanced account of the period (Schmitter, 1998a: 13). As Caporaso notes:

> Court judgements are made on the basis of a simple majority, proceedings are held in secret, and no dissenting opinions are published. Thus, if the court can "find" justification for something in the Treaty, it effectively reverses the institutional dynamics of the Council of Ministers. Whereas the Council has to agree unanimously for a social policy provision to pass, the Court, if it interprets such provisions to be implied by the Treaty, automatically requires the unanimous consent of the Council to reverse it. (Caporaso, 2000: 28)

As a consequence, the ECJ has brought about a 'quasi-constitutionalisation' of social policy. There were two important steps in this process. First, the 'principle of direct effect' caused certain provisions of EU law, particularly Treaty law and regulations, to confer legal rights on individuals. Second, the *Costa* v. *ENEL* case of 1964 set a precedent for the supremacy of EU law over the laws of member states (Caporaso, 2000: 28–31).

Finally, it is worth noting, the European Trade Union Confederation (ETUC) enjoyed some success at this time, briefly raising hopes for continental corporatist bargaining (Streeck and Schmitter, 1991: 138–40).

3. The third trajectory of continental juridification, *consortio*, was marked by the liberal economic ethos of the 1980s. The SEA revived the European project, though the emphasis now lay on market integration, rather than supranational institution building. Distinctions between neofunctionalist and intergovernmentalist approaches were now less pronounced, due to the levelling effect of market ideas and growing economic interdependence (Schmitter, 1998a: 8–11). Nevertheless, differences remained. Against the moderate neofunctionalism of Sandholtz and Zysman (1989), for example, Moravcsik's Liberal Intergovernmentalism depicted the SEA as the outcome of interstate bargains between Britain, France and Germany. The preconditions for this were the convergence of economic policy prescriptions among ruling party coalitions in these countries following the election of the British

Conservatives in 1979 and the reversal of French Socialist Party policy in 1983. Also essential was the negotiating leverage that France and Germany gained by threatening to create a 'two track' Europe that would exclude the British (Moravcsik, 1991: 42).

It is difficult to overstate the importance of Jacques Delors, Commission President from 1985 to1995, to this phase of the European project. His vision of a European Social Model (ESM) raised hopes of combining a dynamic continental economy with the levels of social protection traditionally aspired to by Social and Christian Democrats. The ESM was to offer a source of legitimacy and identity distinct from the Anglo-American economic models then in the ascendant. Yet it was also meant to transcend a purely oppositional relationship between welfare policy and the market. Its aim was, instead, the harmonious interaction of economic growth, employment policy, transnational corporatism and civil society.

4. For Habermas, ratification of the EU Constitution was not merely a way of legitimising the status quo. Rather, it was to open the door to a deeper *political* integration of Europe, ultimately stretching to such contentious issues as tax harmonisation. This would have brought the European project full circle, setting it back on its initial trajectory of *stato*. With the Constitution's rejection, however, post-Maastricht juridification can be viewed as an example of Schmitter's *condominio*. Writing prior to the Constitutional Convention, he noted how this

> would be the most unprecedented, even unimaginable, outcome of all for the Euro-polity since it would be based on variation in both territorial and functional constituencies ... Instead of one Europe with recognised and contiguous boundaries, there would be many Europe's. Instead of a Eurocracy accumulating organizationally distinct but politically coordinated tasks around a single centre, there would be multiple regional institutions acting autonomously ... [resulting] in competitive, even conflictual, situations. (Schmitter, 1998b: 136)

Approved at the Maastricht meeting of the European Council in December 1991 and signed in the following year, the Treaty on European Union (TEU) came into force in 1993, thus running in parallel with the fall of Communism. The TEU was the outcome of two intergovernmental conferences: one on European Monetary Union (EMU), the other on European Political Union (EPU). The TEU appealed to Habermas (1998c: 4) particularly as a means of binding the newly reunified Germany into a network of continental commitments.

The TEU constituted an 'institutionalisation of diversity', suggested Schmitter (1998b: 127), for it replaced the 'Community method', where all member states proceeded at the same pace, with a 'pillar' structure and numerous national opt outs. EU juridification would thereon be characterised by 'variable geometry': the simultaneous activity of multiple integrative dynamics, with variations dependent on policy area and national setting (Mazey, 1996: 35–6). The eventual accession to EU membership of Central European states only exacerbated the complexity of this arrangement, which the European Constitution and Lisbon Treaty have in turn been intended to address.

Once again, theories evolved to accommodate a changing reality. Multi-level governance (MLG) came to prominence as an explanation for the institutional landscape created by the TEU. The originators of the theory, Hooghe and Marks, argued that European integration had shifted certain areas of policy making upward to supranational institutions, while regionalism had effected a displacement of elements of political authority to subnational levels of government (Hooghe and Marks, 2001). Neoinstitutionalist approaches to the study of European integration had also attained a foothold by the mid-1990s (Aspinwall and Schneider, 2001: 1); a range of constructivisms would follow a short time later (Christiansen, Jørgensen and Wiener, 2001).

Delors' presidency of the European Commission coincided with the initial phase of the *condominio* era. His hopes for the ESM were in tune with the cautious optimism of the post-Cold War West, anticipating in some respects the social democratic Third Way that would soon be in the ascendant. Prior to Delors, the Commission's collegiate structure had tended to hamper the development of a single institutional purpose, individual Directorates General (DG) emphasising their sectoral interests whenever possible. Delors endowed the Commission with a social-market ethos (Ross, 1995). However, this had largely dissipated by the time of the constitutional referenda of 2005, and he was unable to infuse other EU institutions with his values. The resulting conflicts exemplified the centrifugal logics of Schmitter's *condominio*.

> [The] revised Luxembourg proposal ... [contained] modified 'social dialogue' proposals to allow the 'social partners' to ask the Commission to 'recommend' to the Council that contractual 'framework agreements' be legally binding across the EC. The new proposals had infuriated the European Parliament, which feared being cut out of the legislative role on which its future was based, and this worried the social dialogue participants ... To both [the European Trade Union Confederation (ETUC) and Union of Industrial and Employers' Confederations (UNICE)], the idea that the Parliament should feel that its legislative prerogative would be infringed upon by a legal 'extension' of the results of collective bargaining implied that the parliament was eager to replace collective bargaining with legislation. ETUC genuinely wanted a European collective bargaining breakthrough and was worried that the proposal might undercut its parliamentary support. UNICE wanted neither legislation nor collective bargaining, but thought that collective bargaining would be easier to stop than legislation. (Ross, 1995: 150–1)

What of social policy? Though the boldness of the Delors era seemed remote by the time the Lisbon Treaty was signed in December 2007, several achievements could still be discerned in this area: a modest framework of positive social regulation had grown from Articles 117–122 of the Treaty of Rome; considerable 'negative' integration had occurred as a consequence of the freedoms of labour and service mobility; and a quasi-constitutionalisation of social rights could be traced to decisions of the ECJ (Caporaso, 2000; Comite des Sages, 1996; Cram, 1997; Leibfried, 2005).

Notes

1   In attempting to categorise the EU, reference to social formations from antiquity and early modernity has been common. Typical of this were Zielonka's (2000) 'neo-Westphalian state' and 'neo-medieval empire', and Engelbrekt's (2002) description of the EU's approach to enlargement as 'neo-Byzantine'. Castells (1999: 363) has also spoken of 'institutional neo-medievalism' in relation to the EU; like Zielonka and Engelbrekt, he stresses external features and institutional form in his effort at categorisation. Habermas goes deeper, equating successive social formations with increases in the rationality potential of the lifeworld. From this perspective, comparisons of the EU with pre- or early modern societies would carry implications of stagnation, even regression; Habermas's (2003a: 369) equation of the Bush administration's worldview with the '"universalism" of the old empires' suggests something of this sort.

3

Integration theory

The EU can be thought of as an outcome of juridification. Yet the concept must be adapted if it is to support more than metatheoretical reflection on the integration process. If the aim is an empirical research programme, thought must also be given to the interactions between national, subnational and supranational contexts that distinguish EU juridification from that of the nation-state. In the case of this study, attention is given to 'Social Europe', the shifting amalgam of welfare states and EU social policy. Established integration theories can be used to refine the concept of juridification. The following section considers which are suited to the task: those indebted to, or at least compatible with, systems theory.

Section two recounts Habermas's survey of action and systems theories. Though critical of functionalism, he has drawn inspiration from the systems-theoretic approaches of Talcott Parsons and Niklas Luhmann. In depicting a complex and somewhat decentralised administrative apparatus, for example, BFN could be seen as the most 'Luhmannian' of Habermas's texts, and thus contrasted with the relative 'Parsonianism' of TCA – it is this sense in which BFN shapes Habermas's conception of the of the EU as a 'complex' polity. This engagement with systems theory was once the subject of sustained debate,[1] yet more recently it has been neglected, particularly in commentary on Habermas's turn to Europe. McCormick's (2007) otherwise commendable study – *Weber, Habermas, and Transformations of the European State* – exemplifies this tendency, containing no reference to Parsons at all.[2]

The early and late works of both Parsons and Luhmann are examined in section three. Between them, four paths of market-administrative development are charted. These correspond with points S_i to S_{iv} of Figure 3.1. 'Systems' approaches to the EU, such as neofunctionalism, can be located along this spectrum. Alternative 'agent-centred' and 'contextualist' approaches are incompatible with the thought of Parsons, Luhmann and, by extension, Habermas; as such, they are to be found on respectively the left of S_i and right of S_{iv}.

Following Christiansen, Jørgensen and Wiener (2001), the term 'constructivist' is used to describe *all* points along this three part continuum. This is to emphasise how each point represents a *compromise* between the

A	S*i*	S*ii*	S*iii*	S*iv*	C
Rationalism					Reflectivism

A = agent-centred
S = systems-theoretic
C = contextualist

S*i* = early Parsons – structural-functionalism
S*ii* = late Parsons – systems-functionalism
S*iii* = early Luhmann – functional-structuralism
S*iv* = late Luhmann – autopoietic-functionalism

Figure 3.1 The constructivist continuum

poles of rationalism and reflectivism.

Drawing on the writings of Geyer (2003), and Christiansen, Jørgensen and Wiener (2001), criteria for the positioning of European integration theories along the 'constructivist continuum' are stated in section four. These are: 1. the role, or lack thereof, assigned to human agents; 2. the extent and site of rationality; 3. the integrative dynamics of a given policy area; and 4. the level of complexity exhibited by it. Hence, integration theories are increasingly defined '*ex negativo*', in terms of what they are not, as they move away from 'the deductive-nomological model of causal explanation, materialism, [and] more or less strong rationality assumptions' of state-centrism (Christiansen, Jørgensen and Wiener, 2001: 4).

In the closing section, analyses of Social Europe are assessed in relation to the constructivist continuum. This pilot survey is intended to stimulate research on other policy areas.

A debt to systems theory

When Norbert Wiener's *Cybernetics, or the study of control and communication in the animal and the machine* appeared in 1948, the topic it addressed was in its infancy. Though antecedents can be found as far back as the Greek philosophers, the development of cybernetics is commonly identified with a series of interdisciplinary conferences held in New York City and New Jersey between 1946 and 1953. The Macy Conferences, as they would come to be known, brought together a group of prominent scholars, among them John von Neumann, Warren McCulloch, Claude Shannon, Heinz von Foerster, W. Ross Ashby, Gregory Bateson and Margaret Mead. At around the same time, Ludwig von Bertalanffy tried to identify 'the common principles that govern open, evolving systems'. Though he distinguished between the two,

Bertalanffy's 'General Systems Theory' overlapped with cybernetics to a considerable extent (Heylighen and Joslyn, 2001: 1–2). The term 'systems theory' is used here to describe both bodies of research.

Systems-theoretic approaches were popular on both sides of the Iron Curtain, though researchers in the Eastern bloc were constrained by Marxist–Leninist orthodoxies[3] (Lewin, 1975: 260). Through intermediaries such as Parsons and, later, Luhmann, systems theory influenced both Habermas's work and analyses of European integration. Luhmann was in a certain sense a 'purist', breaking with Parsons' residual neo-Kantianism and re-emphasising systems concepts such as Ashby's 'Law of requisite variety' (Ashby, 1956: 207; McCarthy, 1978: 224). Thus, Haas (2001: 29) states how by 1964, when the first edition of *Beyond the Nation State* was published, his 'epistemological commitment had become Parsonian', superseding the Weberian orientation of his earlier book *The Uniting of Europe* (1958). Deutsch, who exercised a considerable influence on Haas and other theorists of European integration (Cram, 1998: 41–4), also wrote of how 'fascinating' he had found Parsons' later work (Rosamond, 2000: 187).

For Habermas, however, the lifeworld is exempt from explanation in systems-theoretic terms. Indeed, he has complained that 'neofunctionalists ... wait for a kind of "automatic" development from domestic markets to a Federation of States' (Habermas, 2001c: 127) rather than acknowledging the *political* assertion of European public spheres that would be required to effect this transformaion.

Action theories and systems theories

Action theories are oriented toward hermeneutics. They are concerned with the interpretation of *intentional* human action, rather than mere 'behaviour'. As an example of the latter, Habermas points to

> the movement of a living body ... By describing an observable motion as behavior, we ascribe it to an organism that reproduces its life by adapting to its environment ... [A]n animal cannot be held responsible for its behavior in the same sense that a subject capable of speech and cognition can be held responsible for its actions. (Habermas, 2001b: 5)

For Habermas, action is

> *intentional* if it is governed by norms or oriented to rules. Rules or norms do not happen like events, but hold owing to an intersubjectively recognised meaning [*Bedeutung*]. Norms have a semantic content: that is, a meaning [*Sinn*] that becomes the reason or motive for behavior whenever they are obeyed by a subject to whom things are meaningful. In this case we speak of action. The intention of an actor who orients his or her behavior to a rule corresponds to the meaning of that rule. Only this normatively guided behavior is what we call action. It is only actions that we speak of as intentional. (Habermas, 2001b: 5)

Only in *combination*, argues Habermas, can an intersubjective theory of action and a systems theory of market-administrative integration explain the nature and workings of society. This distinctive approach excludes, among others, agent-centred and contextualist social theories.

The dialectical theories of Hegel and Marx each combine action and systems perspectives. Their failures, and those of successive efforts such as Parsons', have, Habermas suggests, resulted in an ongoing bifurcation of the social sciences.

> In his *Philosophy of Right* Hegel resolved this problem through an idealist transition from subjective to objective spirit. And Marx brought in the theory of value so as to be able to connect economic statements about a system's anonymous interdependencies with historical statements about the lifeworld contexts of actors, individual or collective. These strategies have since lost their plausibility. Thus systems theory and action theory can be viewed as the *disjecta membra* of this Hegelian–Marxist heritage. The older German sociology – whose points of departure were Dilthey, Husserl, and (with Weber) especially the Southwest German school of neo-Kantianism – set out its basic concepts in action-theoretical terms. At the same time, the foundations were being laid for ... the conception of a system steered by the money medium.
>
> The history of social theory since Marx might be understood as the unmixing of two paradigms that could no longer be integrated into a two-level concept of society connecting system and lifeworld. (Habermas, 1995: 202)

Adherents of rational choice theory also assign intentions to the conduct of agents (Habermas, 2001b: 11). Yet in excluding cultural values from their analyses they are left with only a strategic conception of rationality, a 'limit case' of intentional action (Habermas, 1990b: 54–55) beyond which reside the scientific claims of behaviourism.

Parsons and Luhmann

The first major phase of Parsons's career stretched from 1937, when *The Structure of Social Action* was published, to the early 1950s. It was characterised, according to Habermas, by a failure, comparable with Weber's, to explain how the *complexes* of action that are the stuff of social scientific inquiry could arise from the 'private choices [*Willkür*] of solitary actors' (Habermas, 1995: 215).

Parsons rejected Hobbesian conceptions of social order. Instead, he took a 'normativist' approach, combining insights from the writings of Weber and Durkheim. For Durkheim, order grew not only from the constraints imposed by society, but also from the internalisation of norms. Parsons saw 'Durkheim's distinction between moral and causal constraints, between the constraint of conscience and constraint by external circumstances, as a decisive break with empiricist prejudices' (Habermas, 1995: 205–08).

Had it been followed it to its logical conclusion, suggests Habermas, this would have been a promising line of inquiry. Instead, Parsons retained an attachment to the 'unit act' of a single agent in interaction with another, rather than broaching 'the idea of a cultural system of values that is intersubjectively shared from the start' (Habermas, 1995: 214). To explain how monadic actors cohere into a society, Parsons instead looked to cultural anthropology, coming to see a social system merely as 'an ordered set of elements that tended to maintain existing structures' (Habermas, 1995: 225).

Realising the limitations of this strategy, Parsons began in the early 1950s to adopt a systems-theoretic frame of reference. Yet, Habermas suggests, this step was taken without first developing an adequately sophisticated conception of the lifeworld. The result was an overly mechanistic account of social evolution, of which the lifeworld constituted but a specialised component.

Parsons's shift from *structural-* to *systems-*functionalism can be dated to around 1953, when he came to identify 'culture', 'society', 'personality' and the human 'behavioural organism' as cybernetic systems, each with a role in conserving the overall social order (Habermas, 1995: 225–6, 238–9). In Habermas's view, the most problematic of Parsons's four 'subsystems' was society. For the task of 'integration' allotted to it rendered 'unrecognisable the seams that resulted from joining the two paradigms of "action" and "system"'. As a result, the lifeworld was explained in systems-theoretic terms, rather than from a hermeneutic perspective (Habermas, 1995: 238–43). This would mean that there was

> no concrete human individual who is not an organism, a personality, a member of a social system, and a participant in a cultural system ... [with the consequence that] actors disappear as acting subjects ... [and] are abstracted into units to which the decisions and the effects of action are attributed. (Habermas, 1995: 235)

Nevertheless, Parsons retained a significant Weberian orientation from his earlier work: the accordance of 'sovereign status' to culture as an influence on social evolution. Parsons arranged his four subsystems in a hierarchy of influence, with culture at the top and society, personality and the behavioural organism occupying consecutive places below it (Habermas, 1995: 248).

Luhmann took a more radical approach. His 'functional-structural' theory depicted subsystems *themselves* as spontaneously arising responses to perturbations from the surrounding environment (McCarthy, 1978: 223). Dispensing with the 'corset' (Habermas, 1995: 283) of Parsons's four function scheme had two consequences in particular for Luhmann: there was no limit to the number of potential subsystems (now conceived of as institutions with specific functions to fulfil), and his work was unconstrained by his predecessor's cultural determinism.

Luhmann later drew on the theory of autopoiesis (1995). A strain of systems thinking developed by Maturana and Varela (1980), the theory recalls Husserlian phenomenology to the extent that perception is treated not 'as a grasping of external reality, but rather as the specification of one, because no distinction ... [is] possible between perception and hallucination' (Maturana, 1978: xiv–xv). Further features are the treatment of 'cognition as a biological phenomenon ... the very nature of all living systems', and the rejection of a clear system/environment distinction in favour of a 'closed' and 'entirely self-referential' perspective on the part of each system, a 'Leibnizian' view for the present day (Cohen and Wartofsky, 1980: v).

According to Maturana (1978: 39), an organism's 'nervous system operates as a closed neuronal network'. Along similar lines, Luhmann argues that social subsystems form closed networks of communication, each capable of processing or dealing with communications of its own sort alone. Mutual interaction is hampered by the self-referential languages[4] employed by subsystems to coordinate their internal processes, an 'autism' resulting from functional *over*-specialisation. Institutions react to each other in an autopoietic, rather than dialogical, manner, perturbations in their environment caused by the actions of one prompting behavioural self-modifications on the part of the others in response (Habermas, 1998b: 334–52).

Another feature of Luhmann's later thought was the idea of human agents as part of the non-social environment, rather than society or its subsystems. This culminated in the exclusion of action-theoretic residues from social-systems theory that had been initiated by Parsons.

Critiqued by Habermas, Willke's autopoietic neocorporatism attributes a 'reflexive' role to law, the binary legality/illegality distinction acting as a 'catalyst to self-monitored modifications' on the part of institutions (Habermas, 1998b: 344–5). From this perspective, the state could promote harmony among subsystems without inhabiting a privileged position in relation to them. This compares with Majone's (1996) account of the EU as a 'regulatory state'. It also brings to mind the EU's perception of itself, as outlined in the White Paper on *European Governance* (2001).

Juridification and the constructivist continuum

Thus far agent and systems perspectives have been considered. To these, the present section adds a gamut of 'contextualisms'. The three can together be arrayed along a single continuum, as illustrated by figure 3.2. It is labelled 'constructivist' to distinguish it from the poles of 'rationalism' and 'reflectivism' (Christiansen, Jørgensen and Wiener, 2001), and because all positions along it represent compromises between those opposing schools of thought.

The logics of this continuum are implicit, however. And while some can be derived inductively from the approaches along its length, those at the contextualist end of the spectrum remain obscure. A clarification of underlying principles is called for; from these it is possible to derive criteria for the location of European integration theories on the constructivist continuum,

A	S*i*	S*ii*	S*iii*	S*iv*	C
Rationalism					Reflectivism

A = agent-centred
S = systems-theoretic
C = contextualist

S*i* = early Parsons – structural-functionalism
S*ii* = late Parsons – systems-functionalism
S*iii* = early Luhmann – functional-structuralism
S*iv* = late-Luhmann – autopoietic-functionalism

Figure 3.2 The constructivist continuum

and for the identification of those compatible with the concept of juridification. What might these underlying principles be? The writings of Geyer (2003) and Christiansen, Jørgensen and Wiener (2001) offer suggestions.

Geyer has argued for the relevance of 'complexity theory' to the study of European integration. Like systems theory, complexity research is viewed by proponents as a corrective to the 'clockwork' view of the universe and reductionist explanations of social life that are sometimes derived from natural science (Geyer, 2003: 23).

Among the features of a complex system identified by Geyer are the following: possession of a large number of components; interactions between components being non-linear and sometimes circular in nature; each element in the system being ignorant of the behaviour of the system as a whole; the system operating in a state far from equilibrium; the system having a 'history'; and the system being to some extent open to its environment (Geyer, 2003: 22). Because it exhibits these features, suggests Geyer, European integration has been difficult to theorise adequately.

In terms of the constructivist continuum, the gradual onset of complexity can be identified with the positions after point S*ii* on figure 3.2, as Parsons's orderly four function scheme gives way to the multiple logics and unlimited subsystems of Luhmann's work. The attribute of 'consciousness' unique to social systems adds a further layer of complexity to that found in the natural world. This is instantiated in 'signs, symbols, myths, narratives and discourse[s] ... that would be impossible to recreate in a different time and place' (Geyer, 2003: 26). Thus, poststructuralist accounts, particularly Derrida's, that foreground these features posit greater complexity than even Luhmann's later work, which remains tied to concrete institutions and infrastructures.

Underlying principles of the constructivist continuum can also be derived from the work of Christiansen, Jørgensen and Wiener (2001) – two in particular. The first relates to the 'world relation' implied by a given constructivist position. The second concerns the role accorded to language.

With reference to world relations, a distinction is made between 'realist' and 'idealist' varieties of constructivism. The former endows human agents with an epistemic, though not ontological, influence: 'knowledge is constructive in nature, but the existence of the world does not depend on the existence of an agent'. Constructive idealism goes further, claiming that agents have 'both an epistemic and an ontological influence on the known world' (Christiansen, Jørgensen and Wiener, 2001: 4). Positions between A and S*iv* on figure 3.2 can be thought of as constructive realist. With Luhmann's later work begins the idealist segment of the constructivist continuum: owing a debt to thinkers such as Husserl, Maturana and Varela, autopoietic-functionalism and the approaches that follow posit a 'reality constructing' capacity.

What of the role accorded to language? As an underlying principle, it is of relevance to the idealist band of the constructivist continuum. In Luhmann's work, language is of little importance (Habermas, 1998a: 379), yet in the wake of his autopoietic-functionalism, point S*iv* on figure 3.2, follow approaches evocative of Wittgenstein's concept of 'language games' (Christiansen, Jørgensen and Wiener, 2001: 8). These approaches emphasise the pragmatic dimension of language and the existence of intersubjectively shared 'rules' by means of which utterances are meaningful to those in a given context.

> [A] subject cannot follow rules in isolation. If someone is following a rule, it must be at least in principal possible for someone else to check whether she is following that rule correctly; one person's rule-following behaviour is, in other words, subject to evaluation and criticism by another. This precludes any monological account of rule-following, for it presupposes that different people have the same competence and are mutually capable of assessing each other's performance … Thus being able to engage in a language game presupposes sharing a form of life with one's interlocutors … Wittgenstein's language games clearly suppose dialogical relationships among participants in interaction. (Habermas, 2001b: xii–xiii)

Poststructuralist approaches can be found toward the reflectivist end of the continuum. For Lyotard, Wittgenstein's idea of an intersubjective consensus among agents on mutually binding rules gives way to seeing 'language games as essentially resting on a contest, a *différend*, with each player introducing new moves, rather than on consensus and convention' (Habermas, 2001b: 55; d'Entrèves: 1996, 34–5). A disavowal of linguistic intersubjectivity also characterises Derrida's work, which emphasises the aesthetic dimension of language: 'the fictional, narrative, metaphorical elements that pervade ordinary language take on a life of their own … [a] world creating capacity (Habermas, 1998a: xiii). Indeed, in contrast to most philosophical discussions of language, which are 'phonocentric' in nature – privileging, at least implicitly, vocal communication – for Derrida,

> [w]riting counts as the absolutely originary sign, abstracted from all pragmatic contexts of communication, independent of speaking and listening subjects …

He looks to the structural properties of the sign that can be realised as well in the substance of ink as in that of air; in these abstract expressive forms, which are indifferent to the various media of expression in phonetic and written forms, he recognises the character of language as writing. This archewriting is at the basis of both the spoken and the written word.

The archewriting takes on the role of a subjectless generator of structures that, according to structuralism, are without any author. (Habermas 1998a: 178–80)

The underlying principles of the constructivist continuum are illustrated by figure 3.3. The tension between system and lifeworld is also represented.

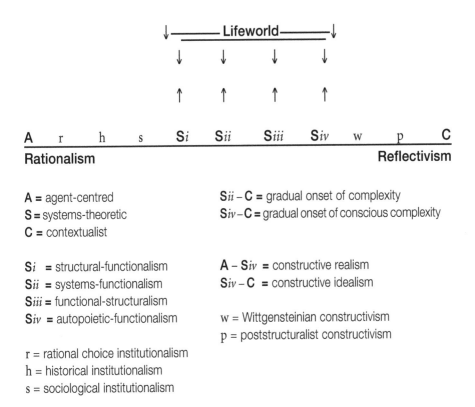

A = agent-centred
S = systems-theoretic
C = contextualist

S*ii* = structural-functionalism
S*ii* = systems-functionalism
S*iii* = functional-structuralism
S*iv* = autopoietic-functionalism

r = rational choice institutionalism
h = historical institutionalism
s = sociological institutionalism

S*ii* – C = gradual onset of complexity
S*iv* – C = gradual onset of conscious complexity

A – S*iv* = constructive realism
S*iv* – C = constructive idealism

w = Wittgensteinian constructivism
p = poststructuralist constructivism

Figure 3.3 The underlying principles of the constructivist continuum

Given the abstraction of the preceding discussion, it remains to clarify the criteria according to which theories of European integration may be situated on the constructivist continuum. These criteria can be placed under the following headings: 1. agents; 2. rationality; 3. integrative dynamics; 4. complexity.

1. Checkel provides a useful summary of the agent-centred approaches of figure 3.3:

> For rational choice scholars, institutions [like the EU] are thin: at most, they are a
> constraint on the behaviour of self-interested actors ... They are a strategic context
> that provides incentives or information, thus influencing the strategies that agents
> employ to attain given ends. In this thin conception, institutions are a structure that
> actors run into, go 'ouch', and then recalculate how, in the presence of the structure,
> to achieve their interests ... For historical institutionalists, institutions get thicker,
> but only in a long term historical perspective ... [Then] institutions can have a
> deeper effect on actors as strategies, initially adopted for self-interested reasons, get
> locked into and institutionalised in politics ... Sociological institutionalists are
> unabashedly thick institutionalists. Not only in the distant future, but in the near-
> term, institutions constitute actors and their interests ... they do not simply
> constrain behavior. (Checkel, 2001: 51–2)

Moravcsik's (1993) Liberal Intergovernmentalism can be found toward the rationalist end of the constructivist continuum, as can Milward's (2000) historical research, and, a little further to the right, the work of Checkel (2001). What of approaches that dispense with the methodological individualism of these authors?

Rather than disappearing at point Si, agency can be thought of as shifting to the level of the social system as a whole, and then, with the later Parsons and with Luhmann, to its constituent subsystems. Recalling the level of autonomy ascribed to institutional subsystems by Luhmann and Willke, Majone's (1996) idea of the EU as a 'regulatory state' can be located in this systems-theoretic domain.

Finally, contextualist approaches to the EU are characterised by a progressive blurring of the system/environment distinction, and with it discernable agents of any sort. What remains is a patchwork of 'subjectless' discursive and symbolic rule-systems (Habermas, 2001b: 16–17). The work of Diez (2001) on the role of language in the construction of the EU gestures in this direction.

2. In discussions of rationality, a strategic-instrumental conception tends to hold sway: self-interested human agents are thought to have a means–end attitude not only toward events and objects in the social world, but also toward the expected intentions and actions of *other agents* (White, 1990: 37; Elster cited in Eriksen and Fossum, 2000: 13). An exception to this view can be found in Habermas's work, where the lifeworld at least is characterised by a *communicative* rationality geared to mutual understanding. Excluding the latter, however, successive points along the constructivist continuum can be defined by their proximity to, or distance from, the strategic-instrumental perspective.

Systems approaches have a means-end orientation yet lack a strategic one. Serving the imperatives of system maintenance, rather than competition between agents, the *functional* rationalities they describe imply cooperative behaviour. Several theories of European integration can be identified with this form of rationality – where these theories differ is the source to which they attribute it. Weber's idea of 'Occidental rationalism' informed the writings of Parsons and Haas; the latter's neofunctionalism, along with other early treatments of European integration, assumed shared European norms to be constitutive of agent rationality. MLG and the regulatory state approach, on the other hand, recall Luhmann's break with Parsons' cultural determinism: the European 'idea' is, from their perspective, but one among many influences on the integration process, while the EU's success owes less to political ideals than to the institutional systems it has developed to cope with perturbations.

Contextualists call even the means–end aspect of rationality into question. For the more moderate among them (Caporaso, 2000; Shaw, 2001; Cram, 1997), however, a 'contextual rationality' (White, 1990: 13–21), recalling the intersubjectivity of Wittgenstein's language games, governs EU affairs.

3. Integrative dynamics are the relationships a given theory posits between the European, national and subnational levels. In the case of Liberal Intergovernmentalism and institutionalist approaches, there are no dynamics to identify, only milieux more or less conducive to the strategic manoeuvring of agents. Declining to specify logics inherent to the integration process, contextualist approaches are likewise exempt from consideration. Hence, the notion of integrative dynamics is only of relevance to systems approaches.

Neofunctionalism portrays the transference of competences from the national to the supranational level. Its initial incarnation (Haas, 1964) in particular recalled the linear model of social evolution put forward by Parsons. MLG, on the other hand, shares features with Luhmann's early func-tional-structural theory, with institutions arising on multiple levels in response to specific challenges faced by the EU – certainly, this integration theory is not characterised by a simple upward transference of competences. Finally, the autopoietic approaches of Luhmann and Willke recall Majone's regulatory state, dispensing altogether with interactions between levels.

4. As Cilliers (2000) and Geyer (2003) demonstrate, complexity presupposes a *system* of some sort. Hence, the concept is not of relevance between points A and S*i* of figure 3.3, where the actions of monadic agents are the object of investigation (this is not to understate the intricacy of the mores constraining agents in stronger varieties of institutionalism).

The writings of Parsons and Haas do not signify the onset of complexity either. Though early neofunctionalism allowed for multiple pathways of inte-gration (Schmitter, 2002: 1–2), its object of analysis was, in Cilliers's terminology, 'complicated' rather than 'complex', possessing 'a very large number of components and perform[ing] sophisticated tasks, but in a way that can be analysed (in the full sense of the word) accurately' (Cilliers, 2000: 3).

It is only after Parsons's systems-functionalism, as Luhmann's influence begins to be felt, that the complexity of the integration processes is taken gradually into account. An awareness of it is demonstrated by moderate neofunctionalists such as Sandholtz and Zysman (1989), who, rather than depicting an orderly transposition of policy areas from the national to the supranational level, suggest the partial dissolution of both levels in a sea of market forces. Adding a subnational dimension and further institutions, proponents of MLG and the regulatory state bring an even greater degree of complexity to their analyses. Finally, as discussed earlier, complexity is at the heart of contextualist approaches to the EU (Caporaso, 2000; Shaw, 2001; Cram, 1997).

Social Europe

It remains, finally, to situate analyses of Social Europe along the constructivist continuum – figure 3.4 does so

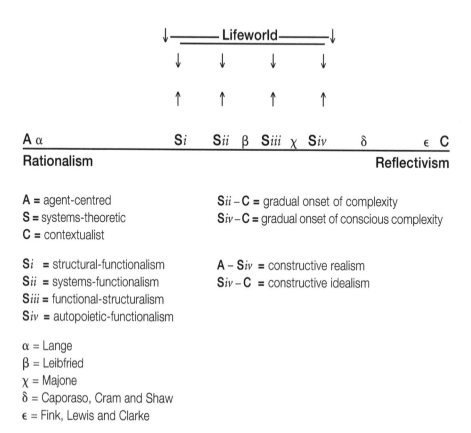

A = agent-centred
S = systems-theoretic
C = contextualist

Sii – **C** = gradual onset of complexity
Siv – **C** = gradual onset of conscious complexity

Si = structural-functionalism
Sii = systems-functionalism
Siii = functional-structuralism
Siv = autopoietic-functionalism

A – **S**iv = constructive realism
Siv – **C** = constructive idealism

α = Lange
β = Leibfried
χ = Majone
δ = Caporaso, Cram and Shaw
ϵ = Fink, Lewis and Clarke

Figure 3.4 Social Europe and the constructivist continuum

Lange's, now dated, 'neorealist' account portrayed EU social policy as the outcome of interstate negotiations. Nevertheless, he saw the creation of the single market as a potential threat to domestic social policy arrangements through a form of negative spillover (Lange, 1992: 226–7).

Leibfried's work identifies a moderately neofunctionalist logic with EU social policy, relating the latter's development to that of the single market (Leibfried, 2010; Leibfried and Pierson, 1995b: 44). While European integration may contribute to the erosion of the welfare state, his argument goes, only a modest, regulatory body of EU social policy arises in its place. In support of this thesis, Leibfried identifies three ways in which Social Europe has been transformed by European integration. First, through positive integration: the development of uniform standards in areas such as gender equality, and health and safety. Second, through negative pressures for welfare state reform issuing from the ECJ, those relating to labour mobility, the freedom to provide services and the impact of the European 'competition regime'. Third, through indirect consequences of the integration process such as social dumping, European Monetary Union (EMU), calls for the harmonisation of tax systems and the single market for private insurance (Leibfried, 2005; Leibfried and Pierson, 2000). Like Sandholtz and Zysman (1989), Leibfried emphasises market rather than institutional integration, logics of dispersal rather than centralisation. A neofunctionalism alive to the disharmonies and complexities of Social Europe, Leibfried's work occupies a position after point S*ii* on the constructivist continuum.

Majone (1992, 1995, 1996) grants EU social regulation significant autonomy from both the single market and domestic welfare states, distinguishing his position from neofunctionalism. Existing to correct market failures of various sorts, the social policy component of the 'regulatory state' provides a stimulus to behavioural 'self-modifications' on the part of the offending institutions. As such, it performs something like the reflexive function attributed to law in Willke's autopoietic account (Habermas, 1998b: 345; Grewal, 2001).

Approaches signified by δ abandon the functional rationalities that can be ascribed to both Leibfried and Majone. Instead, multiple contextual rationalities are suggested (White, 1990: 10). Some depict the EU as the sum of several bodies of 'rules' – legal and institutional – without attempting to encapsulate these in a single theoretical account. Wittgenstein's concept of language games constitutes an obvious precedent for this way of thinking (Habermas, 2001b: 53–4). Insights into the 'quasi-constitutionalisation' of the EU through decisions of the ECJ, and the importance to Social Europe of 'symbolic politics' and 'soft law' are characteristic of this perspective (Caporaso, 2000; Cram, 1997; Shaw, 2001).

Even weak rationality claims are abandoned as rule-orientated approaches give way to poststructuralist ones. The writings of Fink, Lewis and Clarke (2001) – which credit discourses of race, national identity, citizenship and gender with shaping Social Europe – are an example.

As figure 3.4 shows, both Leibfried and Majone's ideas can inform analyses of juridification as it pertains to Social Europe. How might a choice be made between the two scholars? Of the five attributes of EU juridification identified in the previous chapter, Leibfried's work concurs with three: the existence of a distinct European level-of-analysis, complexity and the guiding influence attributed to the single market. Majone, on the other hand, suggests only one attribute: complexity. As such, Leibfried's work is deemed to be of greater relevance to this study.

Notes

1 Indeed, notes Holub, a volume containing 'the long and detailed critiques ... [Habermas] and Luhmann produced of each other's works ... sold more than 35,000 copies, an astounding figure considering the extremely demanding and at times technical styles of both' (Holub, 2006: 69).

2 Does this matter? A claim of the present study is that it does. Habermas (1995: 199) has praised Parsons's work for its 'level of abstraction', an achievement inseparable from its systems-theoretic orientation. He has also written of the 'momentous effort in abstraction' required to foster solidarity among European citizens (Habermas, 1999a: 58). Linking the two statements is the idea that progress, whether in the history of ideas or in politics, entails a paradigm shift, a move from the concrete, 'quasi-natural', assumptions of the status quo to a more abstract conceptual framework. Without acknowledging Habermas's debt to systems theory, it is difficult to see why he has viewed the nation-state as a historically situated, and hence transitory, political form – merely another in a series of compromises between system and lifeworld – against the backdrop of enduring nationalist sentiment in Europe. Neglecting this aspect of his thought has a further consequence: it deprives citizens, policy-makers and scholars of heuristic tools for the conceptualisation of postnational politics.

3 The case was quite different in early 1970s Chile. During the Socialist administration of Salvador Allende, cybernetic principles were applied to the country's industrial economy (Medina, 2006).

4 'Eurospeak' and the vocabulary of Euroscepticism could be cited as examples.

4

Democratic theory

Chapters 2 and 3 were written from what Habermas (1995: 204) refers to as the 'external perspective of an observer'. Like the state and the market, the lifeworld is seen from outside, attention given to its role in the maintenance of social life.

Bringing the reconstruction of social modernity at the level of the EU to a close, the present chapter looks at a second, 'internal', perspective posited by Habermas (1995: 204). The lifeworld's encounters with administrative and economic systems are opened up for analysis. At their worst, such encounters result in the colonisation of the lifeworld by the imperatives of those systems, a process recognised, among others, by Durkheim, Marx and Weber (Habermas, 1995).

Two conceptions of democracy are present in Habermas's theoretical writings. In BFN there is optimism, with the potential for the public sphere, via the parliamentary complex, to modulate the workings of the state and, thereby, the market.

In TCA a different tone prevails. Democracy is thought only to entail resistance by the public sphere to lifeworld colonisation. As noted in chapter 1, Habermas (1994a) coined the term 'reflective welfare state project' to describe this idea of democracy. His views were informed by the rise of the German Green Party and other NSMs of the day. Some of these groupings were seen as being sensitive to the deformations of the lifeworld, effected not only by the economy, a traditional concern of the left, but also by the welfare state. The latter offered shelter from market forces, yet there was no question of it, in turn, being constrained by a layer of bureaucracy – that task belonged to the public sphere.

Both conceptions of democracy can be discerned in Habermas's writings on Europe. In an article on the Constitution (written before 9/11), the sluice gate model of BFN was suggested (Habermas, 2001a). Habermas's favourable account of the mass protests in Europe against military intervention in Iraq, on the other hand, recalled the siege model of TCA, with civil society exerting an influence on the state from outside (Habermas and Derrida, 2003).[1]

The siege model is considered in the following section. One outcome of lifeworld colonisation identified by Habermas is the 'withdrawal of legitimation' (1995: 143, 1998b: 333) from the state. It is widely cited as a consequence of the EU's 'democratic deficit', evident in the widespread decline of the 'permissive consensus', a perception of European integration as an innocuously technical, rather than political, endeavour. Other signs of lifeworld colonisation/the democratic deficit can be discerned in the spheres of personal and cultural life.

The second section deals with the sluice gate model. Against his critics, Habermas has argued that a demos, as generally understood, is not a precondition for EU democracy. Other conceptions of democracy are considered in the third section.

The siege model

The lifeworld, according to Habermas, has three structural components: 'culture', 'society' and 'personality' (Habermas, 1995: 153). In speaking of culture, Habermas refers back to the phenomenological approaches of Husserl and Schutz, where the term denotes the 'stock of knowledge from which participants in communication supply themselves with interpretations as they come to an understanding about something in the world' (Habermas, 1995: 138). Yet, he continues:

> communicative action is not only a process of reaching understanding; in coming to an understanding about something in the world, actors are at the same time taking part in *interactions* [my italics] through which they develop, confirm, and renew their memberships in social groups and their own identities ... processes of social integration and socialization. (Habermas, 1995: 139)

As regards society, the second component of the lifeworld, Habermas has in mind 'the legitimate orders through which participants regulate their memberships in social groups and thereby secure solidarity' (Habermas, 1995: 138). Among theoretical treatments of society, those of Durkheim and Parsons stand out.

Finally, there is personality. The tradition of social theory stemming from Mead is of relevance here, for it 'is based on a concept of the lifeworld reduced to the aspect of the socialisation of individuals ... role playing, role taking, role defining, and the like ... [Hence, it] is only consistent when the theory of society shrinks down then to *social psychology*' (Habermas, 1995: 140).

Table 4.1 illustrates the manner in which the lifeworld is able to reproduce itself over time. Each of its components is shaped by three processes: 'cultural reproduction', 'social integration' and 'socialisation'. Thus, lifeworld reproduction has nine aspects.

What of lifeworld colonisation? With regard to early twentieth-century Europe, Habermas concurs with Polanyi's study *The Great Transformation* (1944) that 'international trade largely freed of political regulation ... had devastating long-term consequences for the "human and natural substance of

	CULTURE	SOCIETY	PERSONALITY
Cultural reproduction	1. Interpretive schemes fit for consensus	2. Legitimations	3. Educational goals, patterns of socialisation (child rearing, etc.)
Social integration	4. Obligations	5. Legitimately ordered interpersonal relations	6. Social memberships
Socialisation	7. Interpretive accomplishment	8. Motivations for actions that conform to norms (internalisation of values)	9. Interactive capabilities (formation of personal identity)

Table 4.1 **Lifeworld reproduction processes**

society," and led, ultimately, to anomie' (Habermas, 2001c: 85). In the vocabulary of table 4.2, the period was characterised by the widespread questioning of state legitimacy (box 2) by radical movements, and the decline of motivation in the economic sphere (box 8), resulting in labour militancy. These phenomena were a reaction to anomie (box 5), as traditional social and religious mores were weakened by juridification.

Writing of the postwar period, however, Habermas diverges from social democratic analyses of Polanyi's sort. Consumerism and the welfare state are thought to have counteracted both crises of legitimation/motivation *and* anomie, though at the expense of pathologies not obviously of socioeconomic provenance.

> [A]nomic conditions are avoided, and legitimations and motivations important for maintaining institutional orders are secured, at the expense of, and through the ruthless exploitation of, other resources. Culture and personality come under attack for the sake of warding off crises and stabilising society ... [first and third columns versus middle column of table 4.2]. The consequences of this substitution can be seen ... [I]nstead of manifestations of anomie (and instead of the withdrawal of legitimation and motivation in place of anomie), phenomena of alienation and the unsettling of collective identity emerge. (Habermas, 1995: 386)

The hollowing out of culture and personality has implications for the individual. The identities of 'worker' and 'citizen' that characterised earlier stages of juridification implied the exercise of political will. Those that have commonly come to succeed them, the 'consumer' and welfare state 'client',

	CULTURE	SOCIETY	PERSONALITY
Cultural reproduction	1. Loss of meaning	2. Withdrawal of legitimation	3. Crisis in orientation and education
Social integration	4. Unsettling of collective identity	5. Anomie	6. Alienation
Socialisation	7. Rupture of tradition	8. Withdrawal of motivation	9. Psycho-pathologies

Table 4.2 Lifeworld pathologies

signify a withdrawal from public life (Habermas, 1995: 350; White, 1990: 109). Where the welfare state is in retreat, it falls increasingly to consumerism to shield the political system from disputations of its legitimacy.

The internal perspective calls for a hermeneutic approach.[2] The rise and fall of Dutch Eurosceptic Pim Fortuyn coincided with the start of the Constitutional Convention in 2002, yet analyses of this conjuncture tend to lack a theoretical framework capable of accommodating both episodes, despite the stimulus Fortuyn's activism provided to the successful campaign against the Constitution. Siedentop's conceptual vocabulary, for example, stretches only to a 'crisis of legitimacy' as an explanation for both the Fortuyn phenomenon and the 'No' votes in the French and Dutch referenda of 2005 (Siedentop, 2005: 26). From the internal perspective of the lifeworld, by contrast, Fortuyn's 'consumerist populism' (Grewal, 2005: 208) and anti-immigration rhetoric could be viewed as the outcomes of 'alienation' and the 'unsettling of collective identity' (Habermas, 1995: 143), lifeworld patholo-gies stemming from EU juridification. As such, the Lijst Pim Fortuyn can be seen to have shared a motivating impulse with the Constitutional Convention, despite the diametrical opposition of their aims: the provision of a *political* response to juridification and lifeworld colonisation.

More gradual developments also yield to an interpretive approach. Goff (2008: 6–7) suggests that the effectiveness of EU Directive 95/46/EC, which concerns 'the protection of individuals with regard to the processing of personal data' and 'the free movement of such data', might be assessed in relation to an 'information-gathering imperative' that has grown exponen-tially in recent years, largely as a consequence of the increasing sophistication of information technology. In particular, a question arises over whether this directive, which applies primarily to information such as bank details and medical records, can challenge the trade in, and amalga-mation of, *aggregated* data (an example of aggregated data would be the consumption patterns of late-night shoppers, considered as a group rather than as individuals, at a particular department store). Such data sets could be combined to yield increasingly refined (and perhaps one day predictive) 'information profiles' pertaining to the behaviours of sub-groups. Utilising aggregated data sets in this way would, despite its impact on individuals, not necessarily fall foul of the privacy protections of Directive 95/46/EC. For the latter pertain to 'an identified or identifiable natural person' (European Parliament and Council of Ministers, 1995: 3), rather than the 'silhouette' of a human subject inferable from the overlap of aggregated behaviours and orientations. Adding to the challenge of enforcing Directive 95/46/EC in such cases is the fact that the information-gathering imperative is *systemic* in nature, rather than stemming from the malfeasance of identifiable persons or institutions. Indeed, Goff's reference to both 'commercial and political information gathering', and the gradual erosion of 'autonomy' and 'subjectivity' that these processes may effect, recalls the colonisation of the lifeworld by market and administrative imperatives, with information technology facilitating a jump in their degree of abstraction, and hence a deeper infiltration of the lifeworld.[3]

In an influential paper, Moravcsik argues that concern with the EU's democratic deficit is 'misplaced'. Indeed, he suggests, judged against 'existing advanced industrial democracies', the EU can be considered legitimate (Moravcsik, 2002: 603). The siege model disputes Moravcsik's case, since, as table 4.2 illustrates, the variegated apathy that results as political energies are deflected onto the spheres of cultural and personal life can actually serve as a functional *equivalent* for legitimacy, despite the resulting attenuation of democratic participation. Viewed in comparison with the internal perspective, a gap in Moravcsik's argument becomes apparent. For while it shares with Habermas's writings an acknowledgement of public apathy and the decline of parliaments (Moravcsik, 2002: 613, 622), the adverse implications for 'democracy' of these developments are left unexplored.

The sluice gate model

A hallmark of modernity is pluralism in the sphere of ethics. In recognition of this, Habermas has developed a procedural conception of democracy that distinguishes ethics from universal standards of morality/justice. The former deals with substantive contextual understandings of the good rooted in particular ways of life. Moral discourses, by contrast,

> aim at the 'impartial resolution of conflicts' and... require a perspective freed of all egocentrism and ethnocentrism ... [This] is simply the 'standpoint from which moral questions can be judged impartially'. As such, moral theory is a 'clarification of the conditions under which participants could find a rational answer for themselves'. (Ashenden, 1998: 122)

As mentioned, Habermas has distanced himself from social democracy in its traditional form. There are both normative and empirical reasons for this: no single ethical framework, social democratic or otherwise, can, he believes, endow a state with the legitimacy it requires; and the complexity, differentiation and efficiency of the economic and administrative systems is such that programmes of nationalisation and Keynesian interventionism (at the level of the nation-state) are no longer tenable.

Procedural democracy is intended only to institutionalise the *conditions* under which citizens may influence the legislative process. The concerns of civil society are to be channelled through parliament. The latter's importance stems from its capacity, when suitably reformed, to facilitate decision making free of egocentrism and ethnocentrism (Habermas, 1998b).

For Habermas, the legitimacy of procedurally generated law means it could have a role in promoting social cohesion in plural societies. This contrasts with Luhmann's view that 'social policy requires comprehensive, nonparticipatory social planning by an administration shielded from party politics and the public realm ... a positivisation of law' (McCarthy, 1978: 229).

Neunreither has pointed out that the conduct of democratic politics at the EU level is impeded by the absence of 'genuine European political parties and European media'. As a result, information on EU activities tends to be transmitted in a nationally biased way (Neunreither, 1994: 300). Along similar lines, Schlesinger and Kevin noted, two years prior to the Constitutional Convention, that even to

> the extent that pan-European media have begun to emerge in the press and in television – and these are still rare birds indeed – their market-seeking behaviour has been the driving force rather than the search for the new public imagined in normative theory. The result is that an elite conversation is now under way in the European space – and much of it is taking place in English [in publications such as the *Financial Times*]. (Schlesinger and Kevin, 2000: 229)[4]

Accounts of the democratic deficit are often centred on the absence of a European demos. This thesis 'informed the tenor of the German Constitutional Court's Maastricht judgement: namely, the view that the basis of the state's democratic legitimation requires a certain homogeneity of the state-constituting people' (Habermas, 1997b: 262). Habermas has countered that

> a communications-theoretical understanding of democracy ... can no longer rest upon such a concretistic understanding of 'the people'. This notion falsely pretends homogeneity, whereas in fact something still quite heterogeneous is met. (Habermas, 1997b: 263–4)

Other conceptions of democracy

Some conceptions of democracy in Europe remain tied to the nation-state.[5] The EU is thought, at most, to command an indirect, 'regime', legitimacy through the tacit acceptance of member state populations (Bellamy and Castiglione, 2000a); however, suggests Offe, its legal-regulatory incursions into domestic arenas have the potential to jeopardise this legitimacy.

> In the absence of a European "people," the demand for accountability will have to be addressed within the framework of the nation-state. Since any attempts by the EU to approach a federal state in its structures and functions will weaken democratic principles, the EU's legal basis must remain grounded in a contract binding under international law, not in a European constitution ... When the borders of nation-states become porous, the functional-systematic and social-moral modes of integration develop in opposite directions. Recent events in northern Italy and the Federal Republic of Germany may be adduced to support this claim. Neither the Padanisian fiscal secession efforts nor the German proposal for a regionalization of the social security system can be explained without reference to the budgetary constraints and competitive conditions wrought by the Single Market ... Habermas vehemently rejects ... this pessimistic view of the prospects for European integration. (Offe, 2000: 79–89)

Some commentators hope for significant levels of 'output' (Scharpf, 1999) legitimacy as a consequence of the EU's efficiency (Beetham and Lord, 1998: 17) and performance of specialist functions, despite the probability of democracy remaining anchored in the nation-state. The idea is not new: since Bismarck proposed state-supported sickness insurance in 1881, social policy, for example, has been a source of legitimacy for states (Parry, 1995: 376). Though only 14% of Eurobarometer respondents approached in 2002, when the Constitutional Convention began its deliberations, associated social protection with the EU, the freedom to travel, study and work, along with the euro – benefits arising from the Single Market – were linked with the EU in the minds of 50% and 49% respectively.[6]

Bellamy and Castiglione (2000ab) have argued that discussions of the democratic deficit rely too heavily on concepts that evolved in national contexts. Thus a rethinking of democracy specifically in terms of the EU would, potentially, yield a less pessimistic account of its current state and future prospects. Yet, contra Habermas, they do not also place a new demo-cratic subject, the European public sphere, at the centre of their argument. Rather, the introduction of fora for deliberation across multiple contexts is thought of as the appropriate course of action given the diversity of public attitudes (Bellamy and Warleigh, 1998: 448).

Finally, for Banchoff and Smith (1999) the presence of *any* dialogue at the EU level, even when it questions core areas of policy, will, in time, contribute to the development of a European demos. Smith (1999: 27–8) interprets the 1997 strike by Belgian Renault workers at the company's Vilvoorde plant, which mobilised sympathetic trade unions in other member states, as the EU's first 'Euro-Strike', despite the fact that many of those involved made, and understood, their case in Eurosceptical terms. The fact that the strike mobilised transnational interests and institutions in this way is taken to signify the growing legitimacy of the EU as an arena for activism and debate.

Notes

1   Habermas sets a precedent for oscillation between books. In BFN he continues to elaborate the 'reflective welfare state project' (1998a: 410, 560n35), a democratic strategy formulated in relation to TCA. The implications of this would seem clear: the discourse theory of democracy explicated in BFN was not meant to *replace* the reflective welfare state project; it was merely *hoped* that, with time and political will, the latter's democratic ambitions would be surpassed.

2   Among the subjects that may be illuminated by the internalist perspective are migration and life in Europe's cities. Though global rather than European in their purview, the sociological investigations of Mike Davis (2004) and Saskia Sassen (2001) are valuable examples of writing on these issues. With reference to architeture and urban planning, Stewart Brand's *How Buildings Learn* (1994) may be read as a response to issues raised by Habermas in the *New Conservatism* – specifically, his criticisms of Le Corbusier. Former Japanese Prime Minister Yukio Hatoyama (2009) has acknowledged the influence of Coudenhove-Kalergi and the Maastricht Treaty on his political thinking; phenomenological analyses of European life in an age of austerity may gain from the work of Natsuo Kirino (2004, 2008).

3   An article by Conservative MP David Davis (2009) covers territory similar to Goff's. Of particular interest is Davis's concern at Google's 'cavalier approach to European legislation', the issues of privacy and information security perhaps prompting a qualification of his Euroscepticism.

4   In the years following Schlesinger and Kevin's (2000) analysis, the *Financial Times* conceded to the taste among its readers for partisan perspectives, to some extent compromising the 'analytical' style that is one of its hallmarks. This shift can be dated to the editorship of Andrew Gowers, which brought Richard Lambert's ten-year tenure to an end in 2001. It was reflected in the array of new columnists at the paper. Christopher Caldwell, for example, has provided a sampling of ideas in circulation among American neoconservatives, for whose intellectual organ, the *Weekly Standard,* he is a senior editor. Amity Shlaes, who contributed as a senior columnist on political economy from 2000 onward, represented the political and economic constituencies of the American right (at times made nervous by the statism and internationalism of the neoconservatives), as personified by presidents Reagan and Bush Jnr, and activists such as Grover Norquist of Americans for Tax Reform. The *FT*'s embrace of 'punditry' – a mainstay of the *Wall Street Journal,* a major competitor – has more recently been exemplified by the work of Gideon Rachman, chief foreign affairs columnist since 2006.

5   Obradovic's (1996) is an especially radical defence of this view.

6   Eurobarometer 57 (2002: 53).

PART II

Cultural modernity

5

Rationalisation

Since the beginning of the modern era the prospect of a limitless advance of science and technology, accompanied at each step by moral and political improvement, has exercised a considerable hold over Western thought. Against this the radicalized consciousness of modernity of the nineteenth century voiced fundamental and lasting doubts about the relation of "progress" to freedom and justice, happiness and self-realization. When Nietzsche traced the advent of nihilism back to the basic values of Western culture – "because nihilism represents the ultimate logical conclusion of our great values and ideas" – he gave classic expression to a stream of cultural pessimism that flows powerfully again in contemporary consciousness. Antimodernism is rampant today, and in a variety of forms; what they share is an opposition to completing the "project of modernity" insofar as this is taken to be a matter of rationalization.   —McCarthy, 1984[1]

This chapter commences the reconstruction of *cultural* modernity at the level of the EU. Attention shifts to the vying traditions – from Catholic social thought to counter-cultural Marxism – that have constituted the lifeworld (Habermas, 1998a).

Habermas's support for the European Constitution was not, as Murphy (2005; Grewal, 2010) has suggested, productivist in motivation. If it had been, EU social policy – particularly Delors' ESM – would have commanded greater attention from Habermas than it actually has. A stronger welfarist orientation on the part of the Constitution would also have been required; yet the latter was a somewhat 'conservative text' (Moravcsik, 2005: 23). In fact, Habermas saw debate on the Constitution as a stimulus to reflection on the 'European way of life' (Jospin cited in Habermas 2001a: 9). Reflection on this scale promised to advance the 'discourse of modernity' – Habermas's *real* aim – in the face of the 'cultural pessimism' that had assailed it for several decades (McCarthy, 1997: vi). 'Europessimism' was but a variant of this malaise.

Modern thought could once be identified with luminaries such as Thomas Hobbes, whose writings marked a break with the Scholasticism of the Christian middle-ages. Now, however, the plurality of ideas and interlocutors present in even the most rarefied of exchanges have rendered the 'discourse of modernity' more difficult to delimit. Indeed, asks Habermas:

is our media society once again undergoing a structural transformation of the public sphere which is inimical to intellectuals of the classical type?

On the one hand, the recalibration of communication from print and the press to television and the Internet has led to an unexpected expansion of the public sphere of the media and to an unparalleled expansion of communications networks. The public sphere in which intellectuals moved like fish in water has become more inclusive, and the exchanges more intense than ever before. On the other hand, the intellectuals seem to be choking on this life-sustaining element like an overdose. The blessing seems to be turning into a curse. In my view this is because the public sphere is becoming more informal and the corresponding roles are becoming blurred. (Habermas, 2009: 53)

Habermas's account of the mythical and religio-metaphysical worldviews antecedent to modernity is covered in the following section. A range of intellectual positions inimical to modernity are then considered; these provide the basis for the examination of neoconservative and neo-Nietzschean tendencies undertaken in chapters 6 and 7.

From mythical to religio-metaphysical worldviews

The lifeworld, according to Habermas, had passed through two evolutionary stages prior to the onset of modernity. The first, characterised by a 'magical' understanding of reality on the part of the individual, accompanied the primitive stage of social organisation discussed in chapter 2. Worldviews were coextensive with tribal memberships, 'the network of a mythical interpretation of the world' lending a 'totalising' quality to thought.

On the one hand, abundant and precise information about the natural and social environments is processed in myths: that is, geographical, astronomical, and meteorological knowledge; knowledge about flora and fauna; about economic and technical matters; about complex kinship relations; about rites, healing practices, waging war, and so on. On the other hand, this information is organized in such a way that every individual appearance in the world, in its typical aspects, resembles or contrasts with every other appearance. Through these *contrast and similarity relations* the multiplicity of observations is united in a totality. (Habermas, 1997a: 45–6)

The lifeworld's second stage of development covered a shorter expanse of time, stretching from the advent of societies organised around a state – that is to say, the first civilisations – to the threshold of modernity (Habermas, 1997a: 201–2). Encompassing the rise and development of the great religions, this stage was characterised by the transition from mythical to religio-metaphysical worldviews.

Following Weber, Habermas (1997a: 214) focuses on the conditions furnished by Christianity for the emergence of modernity in the West. The intersection between the Judeo-Christian and Hellenic traditions, exemplified by Aquinas's *Summa theologiae*, is described as a 'remarkable' occurrence, for these were the 'two worldviews with the structurally greatest potential for rationalisation'. Synthesis of the two traditions also had the effect of refining further their respectively ethical and cosmological teachings (Habermas, 1997a: 205–14).

Until the close of the high middle-ages, however, these elements remained apart from 'profane domains of life and experience' (Habermas, 1997a: 214). The Reformation would change this. Weber examined the process of ethical rationalisation it set in motion.

> The religious asceticism that flowered in medieval monastic orders had to penetrate all *extrareligious departments of life*, so that profane actions were also subjected to the maxims of the ethic of conviction (which was at first anchored in religion). Weber locates this process in the emergence of the Protestant ethic of the calling. By contrast, he shows less interest in a parallel development, the emergence of modern science (without which the development of modern law is also incomprehensible). In this area the uncoupling of theory from the *experiential domains of practice* – particularly from those of social labour – had to be overcome. Theoretical argumentation had to be rejoined above all with those experiential domains accessible from the technical perspective of the craftsman. The solution to this second problem came in the form of the experimental natural sciences. The social carriers of those strands of tradition that were combined, amazingly, in modern science – the Scholastics, the Humanists, and above all the engineers and artists of the Renaissance – played a role in releasing for purposes of research practice the potential stored in cognitively rationalized worldviews – a role similar to that played by the Protestant sects in transposing ethically rationalized worldviews into everyday practice. (Habermas, 1997a: 215)

For Weber, it was the *curtailment* of rationalisation in the realm of ethics, rather than outright disenchantment, that facilitated social modernity. Religious motivation explained the work ethic – 'irrational from the standpoint of self-interest' – characteristic of capitalism (Weber quoted in Habermas, 1997a: 184). This bedrock of motivation and meaning remained vulnerable, however. Horkheimer and Adorno (2002: 1) carried Weber's thesis to an extreme, stating, toward the close of World War Two, that in the wake of disenchantment 'the wholly enlightened earth is radiant with triumphant calamity'. Habermas's comparative optimism toward rationalisation stems from his conception of reason. For if, as he has argued since his 'linguistic turn', rationality is located in the pores of communication, norms and values may arise out of social dialogue, and not only from tradition.

Weber understood the Protestant ethic, a remnant of early modernity, to be incarnated in 'private enterprise'. Parsons cast his net more widely, discerning it in the professions, 'secular callings' such as medicine and the law (Parsons, 1999: 39). More Marxian[2] in orientation, Habermas (1994c, 1998a: 75–82) built on the insights of his predecessors with the idea of 'productivism' as a secular ideology. The continuing importance of production, economy and labour to conceptions of modernity is diagnosed by him as a cause of its present impasse, for productivism's relevance to analyses of society[3] has declined alongside its capacity to stir the 'utopian energies' on which the welfare state and social democracy had traditionally drawn (Habermas, 1994c). In response to these shortcomings, Habermas has looked to the philosophy of language as the basis for an alternative, 'dialogical', account of modernity – 'undistorted, domination-free communication' (Müller, 2001: 46) is its core concept and motivating ideal.

The idea of modernity

Hans Robert Jauss, notes Habermas, has traced the word 'modern' to the late fifth century, where it was used to distinguish the Christian present from the pagan Roman past. It was subsequently employed, with 'a different content in each case', to articulate 'the consciousness of an era that refers back to the past of classical antiquity precisely in order to comprehend itself as the result of a transition from the old to the new'. Hence, not only from the late middle-ages, when the foundations of the contemporary world were laid, but in the Carolingian Renaissance and comparable moments of cultural innovation, 'modernity' was heralded 'whenever the consciousness of a new era developed in Europe through a renewed relationship to classical antiquity' (Habermas, 1996a: 39). As with the '*querelle des anciens et des modernes,* the dispute with the protagonists of a classicistic aesthetic taste in late seventeenth-century France, it was always *antiquitas,* the classical world, which was regarded as the normative model to be imitated'. It was only the spread of the 'French Enlightenment's ideal of perfection and the idea, inspired by modern science, of the infinite progress of knowledge and the advance toward social and moral improvement that gradually lifted the spell exercised on the spirit of these *early* moderns by the classical works of antiquity' (Habermas, 1996a: 39). Condorcet's thought exemplifies this shift.

> [He] interprets the concept of perfection according to the model of scientific progress. Perfection no longer means, as it does in the Aristotelian tradition, the realization of a telos found in the nature of a thing; it signifies instead a process of improvement that does have a direction but is not teleologically limited in advance. (Habermas, 1997a: 146)

For Adorno, the artistic avant-garde that arose in mid nineteenth-century Europe was quintessentially expressive of the spirit of modernity. Certainly, it crowned the liberation of scientific and moral-legal judgements that had already been set in motion by the Renaissance and Enlightenment. This aesthetic mentality was initially evident in the works of Baudelaire and Poe, reaching its 'zenith' with surrealism and the Dadaists of the Cabaret Voltaire (Habermas, 1996a: 40). Philosophically, it found a voice in Nietzsche, whom Habermas (1998a) takes to have broken from the 'subject centred' rationality that had characterised modern thought since Descartes. Like Nietzsche's work, the avant-garde had implications for personal conduct inimical to the Protestant ethic, both describing and celebrating a 'decentred subjectivity', one contemptuous of the constraints and duties of bourgeois life. This bohemian style of art, life and oppositional politics would recur with the counter-culture of the 1960s (Habermas, 1994b, 1996a, 1998a), exerting a residual influence until 9/11.

The avant-garde completed the separation into three distinct 'moments' of the substantive reason that Scholasticism had locked into a single worldview. Each of these 'value spheres' was subject to institutionalisation, thereby giving rise to 'expert cultures' of science and knowledge, morality and law, and artistic practice and criticism (Habermas, 1995, 1997a, 1998a).

Habermas gives particular attention to the second of these expert cultures. Toward the close of the middle-ages, he suggests, the differentiation of morality, law and ethics was set in motion. Deinstitutionalised morality gradually took the form of the personalised judgement of universal principles. Law, on the other hand, was reduced to a force 'imposed from without', 'an institution detached from the ethical motivations of the legal person'. The Reformation, as already mentioned, gave rise to a 'profane ethics of conviction and responsibility' (Habermas, 1997a: 174).

Three conservative types

Ideally at least, the spheres of specialist knowledge that have been liberated by rationalisation are to be drawn on freely in the course of open discussion. In reality of course, public discourse is frequently occluded, certain value spheres and worldviews overshadowing others. In recent decades, Habermas suggests, such occlusions have increasingly been offered as *responses* to rationalisation, providing 'ready made' norms without the need for reflection. Discourses serving this purpose can be recognised by their 'opaqueness'. Habermas has labelled their intellectual progenitors 'conservatives' (1994b, 1996a, 1998a).

The 'left-Nietzscheanism' of poststructuralists such as Derrida and Foucault is described as a 'Young Conservative' stance. This is due to its embrace of the decentred subjectivity of the aesthetic avant-garde, and the accompanying rejection of stable patterns of cognition, work and life – paradoxically, 'an implacable opposition to modernism precisely through a modernist attitude' (Habermas, 1996a: 53).

By contrast, 'Old Conservatives', commonly exponents of neo-Aristotelian and communitarian positions, question cultural modernity in its entirety, prescribing a reversal of disenchantment. This school of thought can be identified, among others, with the political theorist Leo Strauss (Habermas, 1996a: 53).

Finally, 'New Conservatives' are enthusiastic toward social modernity and productivism, embracing liberal nationalism and the scientific value sphere to the extent that these further their aims. Hobbes (2000) can be regarded as a precursor of this constituency, his influence discernable in its scientific orientation toward political thought and its view that a state religion/ideology merits promotion to the extent that it contributes to social order. A belief in social Darwinism – whether centred on individual or group relations (Burrow, 1991: 481) – is also common to New Conservatives, particularly to the extent that they foreground competitive forms of interaction and scientific explanations for social life. Evolutionary psychology has brought these elements together (Edwards, 2003); supporters aim to shape the future direction taken by social research and policy making (Pinker, 2002).[4]

Significantly, Habermas did not designate the three positions conservative in relation to the traditional categories of left and right, but rather on the grounds of their shared opposition to modernity. Hence, among the precursors of the French poststructuralists he placed the 'conservative revolutionaries', right-wing German intellectuals such as Ernst Jünger and Oswald Spengler (Wolin, 1994: xxxn35). Similarly, although New Conservatism was considered by Habermas primarily to be an influence on the centre-right, the centrality of productivism to it recalled his discussions of social democracy (1994c: 62) and state socialism (1994b: 41–2). Finally, he has equated systems-theoretic accounts of social life with New Conservatism, this time on grounds of their technocratic orientations, conceptual debts to the scientific value sphere and neglect of the lifeworld (d'Entrèves, 1996: 4; Habermas, 1995).

Figure 5.1 depicts Habermas's three conservative types. Actors in the political arena tend to be *hybrids* of the latter, residing at various points on the continua between them.

The 'neoconservatives' of continuum iii (not to be confused with the New Conservative intellectuals considered above) are examined in the next chapter.[5] There it is suggested that Habermas *already* sees early signs of cultural modernity at the level of the EU. In the early 1980s, his writings on American and German neoconservatives provided a contrast against which cultural modernity, discussed mostly in terms of progressive tendencies in the FRG, could more clearly be perceived (1994bc). His critical assessment of the foreign policy of the Bush administration performed a similar function, providing the contrast against which a European public sphere could be discerned, at least in outline (Habermas, 2001a, 2002, 2003a, b).

Habermas wrote of other antimodernist tendencies in the early 1980s, yet their successors received little attention in his later work. With this in mind, chapter 7 updates continua i and ii, considering a largely Eurosceptical, yet otherwise diverse, array of actors and movements.

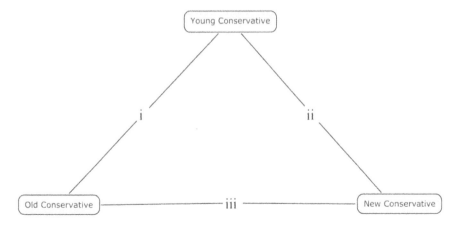

Figure 5.1 Three conservative types

Notes

1 McCarthy (1997: vii).
2 Outhwaite (1996: 5) deftly encapsulates Habermas's relationship with the Weberian/Parsonian and Marxist traditions: 'If Max Weber has been described as a bourgeois Marx, Habermas might be summarily characterised as a Marxist Max Weber.'
3 The following authors are most often quoted by Habermas in relation to this development: Gorz (Habermas, 2000: 32), Inglehart (Habermas, 1994b: 30) and Offe (Habermas (1994c: 53).
4 Steven Pinker's *The Blank Slate* (2002) epitomises the New Conservative position, particularly in its criticisms of the aesthetic avant-gardes and counter-cultures of the previous century. A review by Menand (2002) undermines much of Pinker's argument.
5 As McCormick (2007: 18) notes, Weber's work has informed neoconservative critiques of the *Sozialstaat*.

6

Neoconservatism

> Let's give our Marxist hearts a shock: capitalism was quite a success, at least in the area of material reproduction, and it still is.   —Habermas, 1981[1]

> The end of history will be a very sad time.   —Fukuyama, 1989[2]

This chapter considers the spectrum of neoconservative orientations found along the base of figure 6.1. These are to be distinguished from the Old Conservative[3] and New Conservative intellectuals of chapter 5.

Even delimited in this way, neoconservatism remains a broad category, stretching from advocates of technocracy, including social democrats, to communitarians for whom even social modernity is to be viewed with ambivalence. Generally, however, Habermas has accorded with the use of 'neoconservative' as a term for the centre-right. This is evident from the three elements with which he identified it in the early 1980s.

> First, a supply-side economic policy ... Hand in hand with ... definite reductions in social welfare services. Second, the costs of legitimating the political system are to be reduced. "Inflation of rising expectations" and "ungovernability" are the slogans of a policy that aims at a greater detachment of administration from public will-formation ... Third, cultural policy is assigned the task of operating

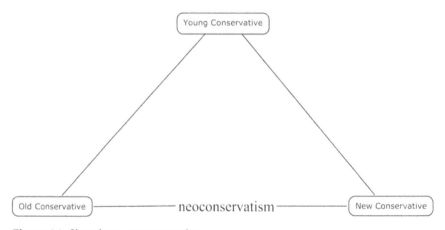

Figure 6.1 Situating neoconservatism

on two fronts. On the one hand, it is to discredit intellectuals as the social bearers of modernism ... On the other hand, traditional culture and the stabilizing forces of conventional morality, patriotism, bourgeois religion, and folk culture are to be cultivated. (Habermas, 1994c: 60–1)

For a time, the economic prescriptions seemed unassailable, attaining the status of orthodoxies among governments of the 'Anglo-sphere'. It remains to be seen whether the financial crisis that began in 2008 will inaugurate a 'new era of statism' in their place (Gray, 2010: 7).

Crescendos of neoconservative mobilisation have coincided with periods of crisis – whether cultural, socio-economic or geopolitical – in response to which they have offered diagnoses and policy prescriptions. The counterculture of the 1960s and energy crisis of the following decade inspired the writings of Irving Kristol and Norman Podhoretz; 'second generation' neoconservatives such as Robert Kagan enjoyed prominence in wake of 9/11.[4] Sections two and three consider the eras of the 'ungovernability thesis' and 'war on terror' respectively.

While neoconservatives have espoused liberal nationalism and productivism, Habermas has called for further rationalisation. The choice for liberal-democratic politics, this would seem to suggest, is either a reification of the early modern political concepts or their transcendence; the third option of Nietzschean disavowal is viewed with alarm by neoconservatives and Habermas alike. Indeed, to the dissatisfaction of critics to his left, Habermas has emphasised the *bourgeois* impulse behind progressive tendencies, such as feminism and the American civil rights movement, that he admires (Habermas, 1995: 393–4).

The ungovernability thesis

In a commentary on his work, Habermas (1996a: 42) described Daniel Bell as the 'most brilliant' of first generation American neoconservatives. Bell argued that the crisis tendencies exhibited by developed societies from the 1960s onward were the offspring of the decentred subjectivity of aesthetic modernity. The result was 'ungovernability', the condition of the Keynesian state apparatus being overloaded by the demands of an egoistic public. Responsible for undermining the Protestant ethic and the social stability underwritten by it, this state of affairs was only considered reversible by means of a religious revival, a hope to some extent realised with the presidency of Ronald Reagan (Habermas, 1994b, 1996a). Against this neoconservative vision, Habermas (1994c) proposed the reflective welfare state project; in the German context, this would be the province of social democrats and progressive elements of the non-communist radical left.

While Habermas shared some of Bell's concerns, he differed in his overall analysis. Habermas blamed consumerism – which had coopted and commodified the avant-garde – for the deformation of the lifeworld, rather than the art world or counterculture. Commodification was, by contrast, under-emphasised by Bell (Habermas, 2003a), due perhaps to a moral-ideological conflation of the market with progress and social cohesion.

Habermas (1994b: 22) distinguished neoconservative intellectuals like Bell from Catholic conservatives such as William F. Buckley, and from the Protestant fundamentalists of the New Right. Yet these constituencies *together* paved the way for the presidency of Ronald Reagan. They shared the aim of undermining the 'Liberal Establishment'; William Simon, treasury secretary under president Ford, for example, called for the development of a 'counter-intelligentsia' to attack America's 'East Coast liberal fortress' (Blumenthal quoted in Keegan, 1993: 57).

> To counteract this Liberal Establishment, which conservatives believed encompassed both political parties, they deliberately created the Counter-Establishment. By constructing their own establishment, piece by piece, they hoped to supplant the liberals. Their version of Brookings [the liberal US think tank] would be bigger and better ... The editorial pages of the *Wall Street Journal* would set the agenda with more prescience than *The New York Times*. (Blumenthal, quoted in Keegan, 1993: 57)

A comparable marshalling of conservative forces occurred in the UK, progressing from the Powellite elitism of the 1960s to the populism of the Thatcher era. A significant juncture was the setting up in 1974, when industrial and racial conflict brought down the Conservative government of Edward Heath, of the Centre for Policy Studies, the work of former cabinet minister Keith Joseph (Keegan, 1993: 61). As in the parallel American case, the cultivation of right-wing intellectuals and journalists was at the heart of this project, with a considerable circulation of ideas and personnel occurring between the think tanks, learned journals, broadsheet newspapers and tabloids. A favoured theme was that of the left and immigrant communities as 'enemies within' (Murray, 1989: 1–7).

Alongside their American counterparts, Habermas considered the German neoconservatives. Yet while he shared with the former a debt to the Enlightenment and to a culture of 'pluralism borne initially by religious sects', this common ground was absent in relation to the latter:

> The German neoconservatives are turning away from ... [Enlightenment] traditions and drawing on other sources. They are reaching back to a German constitutionalism that retained of democracy little more than the constitutional state, to themes from a Lutheran state ecclesiasticism rooted in a pessimistic anthropology, and to the motifs of a Young Conservatism whose heirs could achieve only a half-hearted compromise with modernity. Bismarck broke the back of political liberalism in Germany. (Habermas, 1994b: 45)

The main beneficiaries of the neoconservative turn in Germany were the Christian Democrats; yet Helmut Kohl ultimately earned Habermas's (1998c:

4) praise for his role in the European project. 'Ordoliberalism' – a body of thought centred on the belief that a market order requires the underpinning and insulation from political interference that only the state can provide (Joerges, 2004: 10–13) – had played an important part in the Christian Democrats' development. It is to be distinguished from the ideas of Carl Schmitt and his disciples, for whom the 'strong state' is to incarnate the precedence of the political over the economic (Joerges, 2003: 180).

In a speech given to the Spanish parliament in 1984, Habermas (1994c) again took up the theme of modernity. Since the late eighteenth century, he argued, utopian aspirations had been fused with historical modes of thought, rather than, as previously, with eschatological (or in Thomas Moore's case spatial) ones. Yet with the 'decreasing power of matters of labour, production, and earnings to determine the constitution and development of society as a whole', utopian impulses were gradually returning to the religious sphere (Habermas, 1994c: 53). Fukuyama's, now famous, essay 'The end of history' deals with similar themes, albeit from within a neoconservative frame of reference. Shorn of a transcendental element, it argues, politics would eventually dwindle to the management of techno-economic and environmental exigencies (Fukuyama, 1989: 18).

The war on terror

Against the backdrop of the 'war on terror', the Bush administration's response to 9/11, Habermas would undertake a second critique of American neoconservatism. Preceding this, of course, was the relatively optimistic period inaugurated by the fall of Communism, Maastricht and the onset of globalisation. The intellectual mood of the West in the early 1990s was marked, according to Habermas, by a lack of philosophical engagement with the future, and thus by the return of cyclical views of history that had been marginalised by the French Revolution. For anticommunists, such as the German historian Ernst Nolte, working in the tradition of Carl Schmitt, this spelt the end of the 'global civil war', initiated by the Bolsheviks in 1917, that had carried the universalist ethics and philosophies of history of the early nineteenth-century to their logical conclusions. For Young Conservatives of a postmodernist bent, meanwhile, the curtailment of the latter strands of Enlightenment thought meant the end of two centuries of terror that had grown from their totalising rationalities. Habermas was critical of both views. Those such as Nolte, he argued, tended to generalise the atmosphere of the 1980s to encompass the whole of the century, conflating figures as different as Mussolini and Hitler, Churchill and Roosevelt, and Kennedy and Reagan under the banner of anticommunism. The postmodernists, in turn, failed to note that the appeals of protesters in 1989 for civil rights and democracy were a case of Enlightenment concepts being wielded *against*, not on behalf of, totalitarianism.[5]

Of the four mainstream positions on Europe identified by Habermas (1999a: 56), all but his own cosmopolitan stance bore the hallmarks of neoconservatism. Liberal-nationalist in orientation, 'Eurosceptics' were defined primarily by opposition to the single currency. 'Market Europeans' sought to resist *political* integration, while welcoming the single market. 'Eurofederalists', meanwhile, were concerned to 'transform existing international accords into a political constitution', and hence to build a basis of legitimacy for the decisions of EU institutions. Finally, cosmopolitans saw a federal EU as the 'basis for a future "world domestic polity" to be secured through international treaties'. This polity would, however, be built on the overlapping structures of *existing* organisations, from the United Nations downwards, rather than being constructed *ex nihilo* (Habermas, 2001c: 116–17).

Lionel Jospin was singled out for praise by Habermas, who spoke of the French Prime Minister's 'magnificent speech' of 28 May 2001. Jospin thought of the

> 'European way of life' as the content of a political project: 'Till recently the efforts of the Union were concentrated on the creation of monetary and economic union ... But today we need a broader perspective if Europe is not to decay into a mere market, sodden by globalisation. For Europe is much more than a market. It stands for a model of society that has grown historically.' (Jospin quoted in Habermas, 2001a: 9)

To a significant extent, this echoed Delors' ESM.

> [The] notion of a European social model – a humane social order based upon the mixed economy, civilised industrial relations, the welfare state, and a commitment to basic social justice – had its roots in the Social Democrat–Christian Democrat mainstream of continental European politics. The conviction that European capitalist societies both were and ought to be different was shared in this mainstream. It was also the core of the political project to which Delors had devoted most of his life. In it societies were more than markets, citizenship more than consumption, and government more than an economic traffic squad. People belonged to moralised collectivities which negotiated with one another for the good of all. Citizenship involved solidarity with others. Government, beyond stimulating economic activity to provide welfare, should craft a wide range of public goods, not only because of market failures and 'externalities', but in response to demands of solidarity. (Ross, 1995: 46)

What distinguished Jospin's ideas from those of Delors, however, was the latter's debt to Catholic social thought (Ross, 1995: 16–17). Habermas (1999a: 53–4) saw Jospin (2002) as formulating an 'offensive' variety of Third Way politics. This was distinct from the 'defensive' version associated with Tony Blair, Bill Clinton and Gerhard Schroeder, and with the writings of Anthony Giddens[6] (1998). Jospin's project was defined by the 'notion that politics should take precedence over the logic of the market', and thus in opposition to a neoconservative ethos "which expects every citizen to obtain the education he needs to become 'an entrepreneur managing his own human capital'"[7] (Habermas, 1999a: 54).

In parallel with his reflections on the European Constitution, Habermas again wrote of the American neoconservatives. The latter exerted an increasing influence on the Bush administration after 9/11, challenging the pragmatism and isolationist nationalism that were also components of its worldview (Habermas, 2003a).[8] Echoing their predecessors' interpretations of Nazism, Communism and the counter-culture of the 1960s, American neoconservatives saw *Al-Qaeda* as an outcome of nihilism, a condition against which the United States was inoculated by its traditions of constitutionalism and religious observance. Contrasts between the Socratic and Anglo-American Enlightenments, on the one hand, and somewhat unsubtle accounts of Islamic totalitarianism, on the other, were a recurrent feature of neoconservative discourses at this time. Commensurate with their Manichean outlook was the American neoconservative's foreign policy, geared to exporting the American Revolution by military means.

In the early years of the twenty-first century, Habermas identified the EU[9] and USA with distinctive self-conceptions, those of cosmopolitanism and liberal nationalism respectively. Yet, as the next chapter shows, it would require a contrast with other, 'blacker', streams of thought for the EU to stand out clearly, its contours apparent from the course it was fated to chart between the Scylla of America's social Darwinist Enlightenment and the Charybdis of Europe's neo-Nietzschean traditions.

Notes

1 Habermas (1986c: 116).
2 Fukuyama (1989: 18).
3 Though an Old Conservative intellectual, Leo Strauss's thought has exercised a guiding influence on American neoconservatism.
4 Kagan's influential book *Of Paradise and Power* distinguished strongly between American and European views of the world, coining a phrase that was commonly heard during the presidency of George Bush: 'Americans are from Mars and Europeans are from Venus' (Kagan, 2003: 1). On the subject of the 'Atlantic rift', see also Sinkin (2004).
5 Postwar critiques of totalitarianism owe a debt to the diary of Prussian aristocrat Friedrich Reck-Malleczewen (2000), a work of conservative anti-Nazism more heartfelt by far than Jünger's *On the Marble Cliffs* (1939; see also Steiner, 1970). The first entry alone, from 1936, which chronicles the death and turbulent intellectual life of Oswald Spengler, merits a place alongside the great literary works of its time. The diary also hints at the conceptual problems inherent in conflating Nazism and Stalinism, and of simply explaining the two as consequences of the French Revolution (Reck-Malleczewen, 2000: 53–4, 121), an approach favoured by neoconservatives and postfascists.
6 For a more critical, though still sympathetic, exchange on the Third Way, see Giddens and Hutton (2000).

7 Habermas's economic prescriptions have accorded with those of social democrats, particularly Jospin (2002). As such, he has placed an emphasis on the state as a means of constraining finance capital. Robert Shiller's *The New Financial Order* (2003) poses a challenge to this view, yet from an ethical standpoint comparable with Habermas's own. Sharing with Habermas a debt to the thought of John Rawls, Shiller demonstrates how instruments first developed in the stock market might be made to serve the cause of equality.

8 See also Stephen Fidler and Gerard Baker, 'America's democratic imperialists', *Financial Times*, 5 March 2003.

9 Habermas's political influence ought not to be exaggerated. Nevertheless, a speech on Iraq by Joschka Fischer mentioned the need for attention to the country's 'social and cultural modernisation', terms central to Habermas's theory of modernity (Quentin Peel, *Financial Times*, 10 February 2004).

7

Cartographies of disenchantment

I do not believe there is a single Nietzscheanism.   —Foucault, 1982[1]

Plainly, our makeup is not only linear, but also cyclical.   —Jünger, 1983[2]

Nietzsche's influence is especially discernable along continua i and ii of figure 7.1. In comparison with the neoconservatives of the previous chapter, the 'neo-Nietzscheans' of the pages that follow are tendentious and varied, often disavowing liberal democracy in favour of esoteric or populist causes.

Table 7.1 (overleaf) brings a selection of neo-Nietzscheans together with the neoconservatives of chapter 6 and conservative intellectuals of chapter 5. Alterations have been made to Habermas's original categorisations where these are perceived to have been inconsistent. Antimodernism was initially discussed by him in the early 1980s (1994b, 1996a, 1998a). In light of its relative neglect in his later writings, recent proponents have been added.

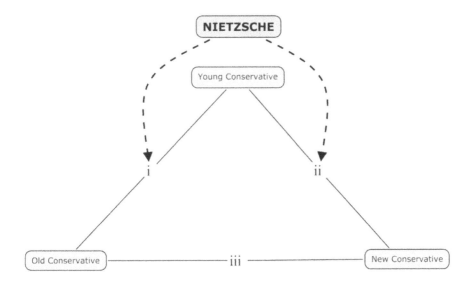

Figure 7.1 Nietzsche's influence

Table 7.1 Antimodernism in the early 1980s and today

	Early 1980s	The global era
Old Conservative	Neo-Aristotelianism, communitarianism	World traditions resistant to disenchantment*
i	Postfascists, deep greens, NSMs, non-Marxist counter-culture, Schmitt,** Sorel*	Postfascists, antiglobal-isation protesters,* NSMs
Young Conservative	Nietzsche, Baudelaire, Surrealism, Dadaism, Bataille, Derrida, Foucault, Heidegger	Students of postmodernism
ii	Benjamin,** Jünger,** Spengler,** Marxist counter-culture, NSMs, market libertarians*	Ballard,* Houellebecq,* Gray,* Fortuyn,* Hitchens,* Huntington*
New Conservative	Productivists, Parsons, Luhmann, 'scientific'/'actually existing' socialism	Productivists, students of social-systems theory, evolutionary psychology,* Dawkins*
iii	First generation American neoconservatives, German neoconservatives, Gray*	Second generation American neoconservatives, non-cosmopolitans of mainstream parties

Notes: * = added to Habermas's taxonomy.
** = relocated within Habermas's taxonomy.

European novels and other relevant texts are considered in this chapter, both as descriptions and embodiments of the zeitgeist – in them are discerned 'cartographies of disenchantment', vying accounts of the causes, consequences and agents of rationalisation. Habermas's Frankfurt School predecessor Leo Löwenthal engaged in a comparable exercise, though with an orientation to social, rather than cultural, modernity.

> Löwenthal's studies of drama and fiction in the nineteenth century served to show in detail that the constraints of the economic system – concentrated in status hierarchies, occupational roles, and gender stereotypes – penetrated into the innermost aspects of life history via intrafamilial dependencies and patterns of socialization. The intimacy of highly personalized relations merely concealed the blind force of economic interdependencies that had become autonomous in relation to the private sphere – a force that was experienced as "fate". (Habermas, 1995: 387)

The following sections look in turn at continua i and ii of figure 7.1.

As mentioned in the introductory chapter, a feature of the Constitutional Convention's intellectual context was the polarisation between 'instrumentalist variants of Enlightenment thinking', on the one hand, and outright disavowals of rationality, on the other. Taking his discussions with Cardinal Joseph Ratzinger in 2004 as a point of departure (Habermas and Ratzinger, 2006), section three considers Habermas's attempt to negotiate a middle way between these extremes. In the sphere of theology, of course, there has been a conflict between atheists – often, though not always, Darwinists, such as Richard Dawkins (2006) and Christopher Hitchens (2007) – and religious fundamentalists of various stripes. English academic John Gray has written of both camps; section three disputes his conclusions, finding them a useful foil for Habermas's more sophisticated account.

Gray welcomes the dismissal of Enlightenment utopianism (2002, 2004a). In its place, he recommends traditions more in accordance with 'human nature', particularly polytheistic ones such as Taoism (Gray, 2002: 79–81, 112–15). The destructiveness of the Enlightenment is blamed by him on its attempt to realise in secular terms the utopian kernel of Christianity. Arguably a species instinct inherent in all human beings, religiosity, he suggests, is of value as a *counterweight*, not complement, to rationality. Yet Gray's analysis stems from a scientism comparable with that of both Dawkins and Hitchens: he differs from the two Darwinists only in residing slightly closer to the Young Conservative position, for which claims to disinterested rationality are merely masks for the 'will to power'. The reductionism of Gray's approach is evident from his conflation of the Enlightenment's heirs – whether Leninists, neoliberals or neoconservatives – with religious fundamentalists,[3] all of whom are understood to be utopians, and hence quintessentially 'modern' (Gray, 2003). Habermas's account of modernity and its pathologies yields a more accurate picture. And rather than a means of re-enchantment, Habermas looks to religion as a cognitive resource in the effort to carry modernity forward again.

The chapter concludes with a diagrammatic representation of tendencies and configurations critical of modernity.

Counter-Enlightenment radicalism

The movements associated with continuum i of figure 7.1 range from post-fascists, such as the French *Nouvelle Droite* (Goodrick-Clarke, 2002: 69–70; Habermas, 1994b: 33), to NSMs critical of globalisation on grounds ranging from social justice to 'deep green' environmentalism.[4] Dissociating themselves from modernity, with perhaps the exception of its aesthetic avant-garde, these movements at times blur the distinctions between left and right. Indeed, they rival their nineteenth-century predecessors in the extent to which precapitalist forms of life inspire their, decreasingly Marxian, anticapitalism (Habermas, 1995: 393).

Some have come to supplement, and even replace, socialist ideas with varieties of 'anarchical mysticism' (Mendieta, 2002: 1).[5] Mystical and millenarian views have also been adopted on the radical right (Goodrick-Clarke, 2002), as have elements of leftist thought such as that of Gramsci (van Kranenburg, 1999). From diametrical opposition in the Cold War, radical left and right have come tacitly to exhibit a circular, perhaps symbiotic, relationship, united in their opposition to the social modernity of the EU, and globalisation more generally.

Differences in political alignment are perhaps better understood in terms of the *ratios* of Young and Old Conservative beliefs adhered to. Leftists incline toward the former (Bey, 1994), while 'mystical fascists' are more enamoured of the premodernism of the Old Conservative position, with its refusal of disenchantment. Paganism has appealed to both sides, perhaps due to the universalism of the Abrahamic alternatives.

The movements located along continuum i also vary in the inspirations for, though not the extent of, their opposition to the EU. Those closer to Young Conservatism (Bey, 1994) lean toward idealised collectivist and egalitarian, sometimes primitive, forms of life in opposition to the EU's impersonal market-administrative structures. Those gravitating toward Old Conservatism, on the other hand, look to the empires of antiquity, medieval Christendom/Islam or folk nationalisms for authoritarian closure (Goodrick-Clarke, 2002) – the traditional stage of social organisation, in which the economy was yet to be differentiated out beyond the sphere of the state, is looked to with nostalgia; in an argument that recalls both Carl Schmitt and Georges Sorel (Habermas, 1994f: 137), Obradovic (1996) has claimed that the EU lacks legitimacy because it lacks a founding myth.

The dark and the black

> They are no philosophical race – these English: Bacon signifies an *attack* on the philosophical spirit in general, Hobbes, Hume and Locke a debasement and devaluation of the concept 'philosopher' for more than a century ... in their struggle against the English mechanistic stultification of the world, Hegel and Schopenhauer were (with Goethe) of one accord ... What is lacking in England and always has been lacking ... – real *power* of spirituality, real *depth* of spiritual insight, in short philosophy. – It is characteristic of such an unphilosophical race that they should cling firmly to Christianity: they *need* its discipline if they are to become 'moral' and humane.   —Nietzsche, 1886[6]

The "dark" writers of the bourgeoisie, such as Machiavelli, Hobbes, and Mandeville ... still thought in a constructive way; and there were lines leading from their disharmonies to Marx's social theory. The "black" writers of the bourgeoisie, foremost among them the Marquis de Sade and Nietzsche, broke these ties.   —Habermas, 1985[7]

In comparison with continuum i, the combination of elements comprising the worldviews of those found along continuum ii has been subject to a greater degree of change. The prevalence of productivism, whether Marxist or liberal in form,[8] rather than science as the complement to the aesthetic avant-garde that was the norm in the postwar era has come to be reversed. Advances in genetic[9] and information technologies, in particular, have captured the popular imagination in much the way that neo-Marxism did after World War Two and the free market did in the Reagan–Thatcher era.

A further development has also affected continuum ii: while the counterculture's ethos of transgression has survived, sometimes in opposition to the perceived censoriousness of pro-integration elites, the liberationist aspirations that once accompanied it have given way to a nihilistic stance. The failure of the counterculture to resist its own commodification, and hence pacification, have no doubt contributed to this.[10] Further, though natural science has filled the space once occupied by philosophy, it has brought in its wake disenchantment and angst. Hence, while elements along continuum i look wistfully to antiquated worldviews and forms of life as panaceas for the present, those along continuum ii are more sophisticated in their disavowals of modernity, declining conservative utopias in favour of a 'consumerist pessimism'. Perhaps ironically, they stem from the transnational bourgeois strata spoken of by Schmitter as a potential 'agent' of the European project, rather than the 'coalition of losers' – a fitting, if unfortunate, epithet for continuum i – he sees as naturally antipathetic to it (Schmitter, 2000: 128–30).

Novels by J.G. Ballard (2000) and Michel Houellebecq (2001) published in the years prior to the Constitutional Convention depict the 'alienation', 'anomie' and even 'psychopathologies' that have afflicted Europe's bourgeois milieux as a consequence of the growing social and scientific complexity of everyday life. As explained in chapter 4, the aforementioned maladies are, along with the 'withdrawal of legitimation' more familiar to scholars of European integration, but three of those are spoken of by Habermas (1995: 143) as outcomes of lifeworld colonisation. Together they add detail to Schmitter's (2000: 128) diagnosis of the 'morbidity symptoms' evident in contemporary European politics.[11]

In its almost scientific detachment, Ballard's unsettling depiction of European corporate life in *Super-Cannes* (2000) is evocative of the observer perspective of systems theory. Elements of surrealism and scientific discourse are instantiated in the prose style and the decentred subjectivities of the protagonists, one of whom remarks coolly that once 'you dispense with morality the important decisions become a matter of aesthetics' (Ballard, 2000: 255), echoing Habermas's warning against a comparable populist 'aestheticization of politics' (Duvenage, 2003: 63; Habermas, 1998c: 4).

Held together by surveillance technologies and private security firms, rather than civic engagement, the bleak, yet orderly, 'gated communities' of corporate and technocratic elites that are a feature of Ballard's late novels (1996, 2000) recall the 'Singapore model' of society written of by Zolo more than the European public sphere hoped for by Habermas:

> In today's world, no more perfect example could be found of the modern *antipolis*, characterised as it is by the highest technological efficiency, extensive use of information instruments, widespread prosperity, excellent public services (especially schools and hospitals), high levels of employment, efficient and enlightened bureaucracy, social relations aseptically mediated by exclusive functional requirements and a total lack of political ideologies or public discussion. (Zolo, 1992: 184)

Ernst Jünger's *Eumeswil* (1977) describes a comparable social system, though this is located in an imaginary future. Combining elements from myriad civilisations, Jünger's vision has parallels with Zielonka's (2000) anachronistic conception of the EU as neo-medieval empire, while also recalling the postdemocratic contours of McCormick's (2007) *Sektoralstaat*.

Though placed by Habermas in the company of Young Conservatives such as Heidegger, the author finds greater affinities between Jünger and a group of writers identifiable with continuum ii of figure 7.2 (see Appendix): like Ballard and Houellebecq, Jünger's qualified embrace of science and technology distinguishes him from the more critical stance of Heidegger (1977) and other conservative contemporaries (Wolin, 1993: 120). Nevertheless, Jünger and Heidegger can be thought of as Nietzsche's authoritarian heirs, rather than belonging to the 'anarchist' path of succession that leads from Bataille to the poststructuralists (Habermas, 1998a: 214).[12]

More than Ballard or Jünger, Houellebecq dramatises the internal perspective of the lifeworld, particularly the discontents of the middle class. In *Atomised* (1998), the travails and neuroses of Bruno, a failed libertine, are blamed on the rapid social changes of the postwar era – particularly consumerism and multiculturalism (especially to the extent that it legitimises Islam) – which provoke his unreserved scorn, and, recalling Durkheim (1951), condemn his brother Michel inexorably to suicide.[13]

Pessimistic theses comparable with those of Houellebecq have been simplified and distilled into a popular philosophy by English historian of ideas John Gray (2002, 2004a). If the plaudits of liberal reviewers – from George Soros and Will Hutton to David Marquand and Ballard (a friend and admirer)[14] – are anything to go by, Gray can lay claim to codifying the cultural mood in the wake of 9/11.

More a gathering of mavericks than political movements, discernment is required to correctly place those found between the poles of Young and Old Conservatism. Figure 7.2 is intended to illuminate the terrain.

Those closest to the Young Conservative pole bear out Weber's warning

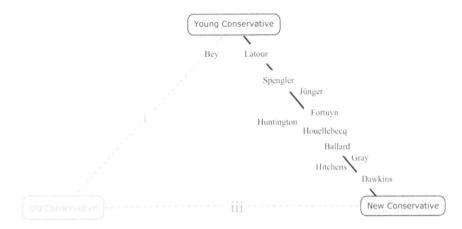

Figure 7.2 The dark and the black

of the rise of a new form of 'animism', as scientific rationality is reduced in status to merely one of the vying 'gods and demons' of modernity (Habermas, 1997a: 246). Bruno Latour's (1993) sociology of science takes for granted such a development. Though located on continuum i, Hakim Bey's (1994) anarchism also features in figure 7.2, essentially to underscore the affinities between it and, despite their secular cast, the ideas of Latour and poststructuralists such as Deleuze.

More than Ballard, Houellebecq or Jünger, Gray's empiricism pulls him toward the New Conservative end of the spectrum.[15] Nevertheless, he shares with the Young Conservatives, among other things, an affinity for Eastern and pre-Socratic thought (Gray, 2002). In line with his earlier neoconservatism, Gray concurs with figures such as Bell (1996) and Blond (2010) on the need for a religious revival if Western societies are to stem the morbidity symptoms that are perceived to have afflicted them. To this end, he has suggested an amalgam of moderate Christianity and New Age spirituality.[16]

Closer than Gray to the New Conservatism of figures such as Dawkins, Hitchens is also pulled toward the American neoconservatives by his support for military intervention in Iraq. His reluctance fully to disavow his Marxist past can be compared with Fortuyn's (Glazov, 2003).[17]

What of attitudes toward the European project? Where Euroscepticism arises along continuum ii – in the case of Fortuyn, for example – it tends to be articulated as a defence of personal liberties, rather than through an organicist form of nationalism,[18] though a somewhat kitsch variation on Spengler's[19] 'Faustian' conception of Western destiny may also be a feature of it. Huntington's warning of a potential *Clash of Civilisations* (1996) was especially influential in the wake of 9/11: an American essay – hence its empirical, rather than 'Goethean', orientation – in the discipline of cultural morphology, it bears the imprint of Spengler's *The Decline of the West*

(1918). Like Fortuyn, Huntington saw the USA rather than EU as a bastion of liberty.

Jünger was enthusiastic toward European unification, speaking of it as an antidote to the baleful effects of nationalism (Hervier, 1995: 126–7). In this, and being influenced by Nietzsche and Spengler, he can be compared with Count Coudenhove-Kalergi, author of the widely influential *Pan-Europa* (1923), though the latter was also an admirer of American President Woodrow Wilson.[20] What distinguished Jünger from countrymen such as Reck-Malleczewen (2000) and Kohl, meanwhile, was a tendency toward the aestheticisation politics, an impulse that Habermas (1998c: 4) praised Kohl for resisting.[21]

Ballard and Gray can also be placed in the Europhile camp, the scientific attitude underpinning their, quintessentially English, pessimism precluding sentimental attachments to the nation-state.[22] In this respect, Houellebecq – widely known for his provocative depictions of multiculturalism – represents a transitional stage between the populist nationalism of Fortuyn and the 'cosmopolitan misanthropy' of the two Englishmen. Ballard called for a deepening of Britain's EU membership, partly as a check on xenophobic tendencies (Wakefield, 2001), while Gray (2004a: 179–86) thought the country's increased involvement might actually be harmful to the European project (understood as an alternative to Anglo-American capitalism), and thus that, 'For Europe's Sake', it ought to remain outside the eurozone.

As already mentioned, arguably the most prominent *political* incarnation of these Young and New Conservative currents at the time of the Constitutional Convention was Fortuyn.[23] His programme was characterised by neoliberal Euroscepticism, an opposition to further immigration and multiculturalism, and a defence of Dutch traditions of personal liberty, particularly in the face of perceived threats from Islam. Only in his emphasis on capitalism, rather than science, did Fortuyn diverge from the thought of the writers above, the New Conservative component of his worldview closer to that of the early 1980s[24] than of today. Though his consumerist populism would no doubt prompt the opprobrium of Ballard and Gray, it also exemplified, and contributed to, the triumph of commodified pleasures over 'public reason' depicted in their works. As such, it bore out Habermas's critique of neoconservative analyses of the aesthetic avant-garde to the effect that the latter is socially corrosive when commodified, rather than in and of itself (Habermas, 1994b).[25]

The cognitive substance of religion

In 2004, Habermas met with Cardinal Joseph Ratzinger, the soon to be Pope, for a dialogue on social and religio-philosophical matters. The interlocutors surprised those in observance with the extent of their agreements and their attempt to chart a middle way between the spheres of rationalism and faith[26]

(Schuller, 2006: 8, 16). Public discussion at the time seemed otherwise to be characterised by conflict, between the incommensurable worldviews of Darwinists and religious fundamentalists, for example. Gray cast himself as a voice of moderation, praising the theological sensitivity of Habermas's work (Gray, 2004b). Yet, in its essential scientism, Gray's outlook had much in common with those of the Darwinists. Rather than justify his faith in science – sociobiology, for example – he resorted to 'common sense' disavowals of philosophical alternatives such as idealism and poststructuralism (Gray, 2002: 52–5), a strategy increasingly common after the publication of Sokal and Bricmont's *Intellectual Impostures* (1997).

Gray's work provides a useful foil for Habermas's. What distinguishes the former from the latter is its mode of engagement with theological issues. Influenced by Hobbes (2000), Gray has an essentially instrumentalist conception of religion: at best, it is a palliative for life's disquieting mysteries; at the level of society, it may offer the state a source of legitimacy, while also contributing to social cohesion. It is as a *buffer* against the 'will to power' and the 'survival of the fittest', the insights of Nietzsche and Spencer, that religion is of value, and at the service of its proper, perhaps genetically ordained, purpose. When, by contrast, the religious impulse is made to serve utopian goals it is pathologically distorted (Gray, 2007). The accompanying mindset, argues Gray, is fundamentally modern; it is common both, he claims, to American neoconservatives and the Islamic radicals of *Al-Qaeda* (2003). Yet it is possible to see in the life and writings of Sayyid Qutb, an ideological progenitor of *Al-Qaeda*, a cartography of disenchantment comparable with those of continuum i of figure 7.1. Qutb lamented the materialism and individualism he encountered in America, dreading their appearance in the Islamic world (Wright, 2006: 7–24). In this sense, the *antimodernist* orientations of Qutb and *Al-Qaeda* are, contra Gray, unmistakable, and certainly stronger than those of the market-oriented American neoconservatives, though Gray places all in the category of 'utopians' (2003).

While Gray looks to religion for a selective 're-enchantment' of modern life, Habermas adopts a different approach. Theology is treated by him as a legitimate mode of thought in itself, despite its inherently speculative character. Its role is not foremost the provision of norms, but that of making available the 'cognitive substance' of religion as the basis for a rationality that is more than instrumental:

> It would not be rational to reject out of hand the conjecture that religions – as the only surviving element among the constitutive building-blocks of the Ancient cultures – manage to continue and maintain a recognized place within in the differentiated edifice of Modernity because their cognitive substance has not yet been totally exhausted. There are at any rate no good reasons for denying the possibility that religions still bear a valuable semantic potential for inspiring other people beyond the limits of the particular community of faith, once that potential is delivered in terms of its profane truth content. (Habermas, 2008c: 20)

Mapping antimodernism

Figure 7.3 brings together themes from the preceding reflections on modernity and its critics. In order to facilitate empirical research, heuristic principles are drawn from the earlier considerations of representative individuals and movements. Habermas, it can be seen, occupies a space equidistant from continua i, ii and iii; his affirmative account of modernity combines elements – liberal democracy, the critique of the subject and the cognitive substance of religion – embraced only selectively by antimodernists.

Continuum ii adds a 'pragmatic' form of Europeanism to the market variety critiqued by Habermas (1999a: 56). Mark Leonard's work exemplifies the former, treating the EU essentially as an *instrument* of interstate coordination. The EU bears comparison, he suggests, with the VISA network, a decentralised, skeletal, yet collaborative structure utilised by the financial institutions that are its members (Leonard, 2005). Thus, transnational administrations – like markets in the work of Hawken, Lovins and Lovins (1999: 261) – are, from this perspective, analagous to technologies.

A number of Eurosceptical orientations are also represented by figure 7.3. The populist variety characteristic of continuum ii most obviously recalls Fortuyn; a nearby reference to 'consumerism, pornography and celebrity' is intended to encapsulate the socio-political and media landscape traversed not only by him, but also by the likes of the British Eurosceptic and former chat show host Robert Kilroy-Silk, and Italian Prime Minister Silvio Berlusconi, figures otherwise closer to the neoconservatism of continuum iii. Even more than the latter, Fortuyn's flamboyance and libertinism were integral to, and not merely afforded by, the power he wielded; only in the developed West, he maintained, in a state famed for its defence of personal liberties, could a figure such as he, a sort of 'Occidental dandy', escape the strictures of tradition.[27]

Against populist Euroscepticism and the mainstream variety that is a feature of party politics and discussion in all member states, continuum i identifies two further types. 'Folk' Euroscepticism stems from the sort of organicist nationalism common not only to Eurofascist discourses but those of authoritarian conservatives as well; it is to the latter, particularly figures such as G.K. Chesterton, that Phillip Blond (2010), a researcher affiliated to the British Conservative Party, looks for inspiration. 'Deep' Euroscepticism, meanwhile, gazes even further into the past, commending tribal forms of consciousness and belonging.

Traits identifiable with the three continua are listed under the following headings: 'Counter-Enlightenment', 'Cynical Enlightenment' and 'Conservative Enlightenment'. The derivation of these traits – the 'political occultism/ esotericism' (Goodrick-Clarke, 2002; Wright, 2006) of Counter-Enlightenment radicals, for example – sometimes entails a departure from mainstream political theory.

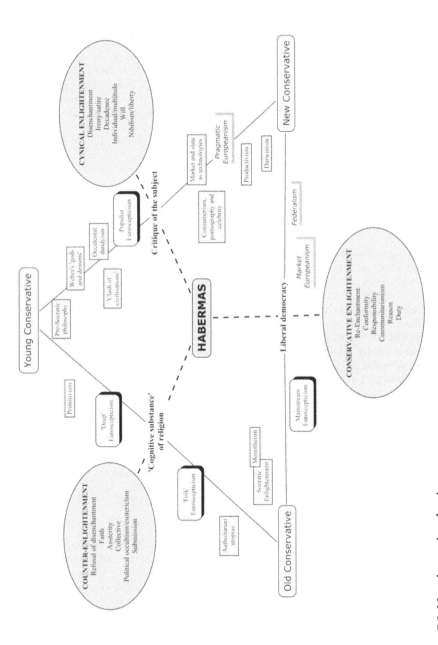

Figure 7.3 Mapping antimodernism

Notes

1 Foucault (1990: 31).
2 Jünger (1993: 43).
3 What distinguishes Habermas's analyses from those of researchers such as Gray and Versluis is that they are not merely descriptive, but also engage with the underlying conceptual structures of modernity. To its credit, Versluis's account of antimodernism goes beyond the customary selection of individuals and movements, making reference to figures as diverse as Rajneesh and the Unabomber (2006: 125, 109). It remains, however, unsubtle. In response to its shortcomings, Luke (2006) provides a more sopisticated taxonomy, introducing terms such as 'amodern', 'anamodern', 'abmodern' and 'antemodern'; nevertheless, his emphasis is still on surface description.
4 The increasing prevalence of such views has been reflected in the editorial policy of the journal *Telos*. Initially oriented toward neo-Marxist scholarship, including Habermas's (1981a), *Telos* has, from the early 1990s, featured writings on or by thinkers of the palingenetic New Right such as Alain de Benoist.
5 This process was already in evidence in the 1960s, and perhaps earlier. Nevertheless, it has grown in prevalence with the waning of NSMs.
6 Nietzsche (1990: 183–4).
7 Habermas (1998a: 106).
8 These constituencies have received little detailed examination in Habermas's writings. They enjoy greater prominence, and hence scrutiny, in the American context (Micklethwait and Wooldridge, 2004). Nevertheless, Habermas does occasionally make reference to them – as 'the handful of jokers who tried to have fun at the interface between a chubby neo-liberalism and a pallid post-modernism', for example (Habermas, 1998c: 5).
9 Houellebecq (1998), German philosopher Peter Sloterdijk (Müller, 2001: 45) and, more sombrely, John Gray (2002, 2004: 24–32) are but three examples. For an insight into the political presuppositions of evolutionary psychology, see Edwards (2003).
10 On the subject of consumerism, Habermas wrote:

> I share Adorno's reservations about mass culture, against Benjamin's overhasty hopes for its 'profane illuminations', only to the extent that the fusion of high and trivial culture has, up till now, fallen short of its programmatic goal. Desublimated mass-art does not penetrate in a transforming, illuminating and liberating way into life-forms reified by capitalism, and deformed and distorted by consumerism and bureaucracy, but rather helps to advance these tendencies. It was not the hopes of the surrealists which were false, but their path – the *Aufhebung* of aesthetic illusion – was counter-productive. (Habermas, 1986c: 173)

A case stronger, and perhaps more naive, than Benjamin's is made by Marcus:

> punk was most easily recognisable as a new version of the old Frankfurt School critique of mass culture ... But now the premises of the old critique were exploding out of a spot no one in the Frankfurt School, not Adorno, Herbert Marcuse, or Walter Benjamin, had ever recognised: mass culture's pop cult heart. (Marcus, 1989: 70)

11 Though unrelated, the assassinations of Pim Fortuyn (2002), his friend Theo van Gogh (2004) and Serbian Prime Minister Zoran Ðinðic (2003), a former student of Habermas's, along with the murder of Swedish Minister for Foreign Affairs Anna Lindh (2003), brought an atmosphere of menace to European politics around the

time of the Constitutional Convention. Rather than enhancing Europe's moral standing in relation to the USA, the images of prisoner abuse at Abu Ghraib that emerged in 2004 only served further to darken the mood.

12 The authoritarian/anarchist distinction is not always clear, however. Jünger, for example, expressed great interest in hallucinogenic drugs (Hervier, 1995: 42–3), a subject commonly associated with the counterculture. More recently, Shimon Naveh, director of the Israeli Defence Force's Operational Theory Research Institute, acknowledged debts to countercultural theorists such as Deleuze and Guattari, Bataille and the Situationists (Weizman, 2006: 8–16, 20).

13 Though unwarranted in its gloom, the reference to France's 'sliding slowly, ineluctably, into the ranks of the less developed countries' made in the prologue to Houellebecq's *Atomised* (1998) is reflected in the declining importance of the École Nationale d'Administration. Previously, a seedbed for France's political, administrative and business elites, its curriculum and training methods have come to be perceived as somewhat provincial (Jo Johnson, 'Caste Out', *Financial Times* 17 December 2004).

14 A sample of reviewers quoted on the front and back covers of *Straw Dogs* (Gray, 2002).

15 This is not to say that Gray's later (rather than earlier, academic) writing is devoid of aesthetic 'effects'. On the contrary, it is characterised by a 'cataclysmic' style that bears debts or resemblances to, among others, the following: Ballard (1967), Golding (1961, 1986), Lovelock (2007) and Rees (2003).

16 These opinions were put forward by Gray during a public lecture in London (5 May 2005).

17 For much of the postwar era, the goal of 'democratic socialism' inspired and mobilised intellectuals of the non-totalitarian left. The concept's exhaustion was finally evident in the wake of 9/11 when Christopher Hitchens broke publicly from his former comrade Noam Chomsky over the latter's response to the event, a schism repeated many times over on the left.

18 Integral to this politics is alarm at a 'youth bulge' in the Islamic world, with the latter's 'angry young men' threatening to overwhelm Europe's ageing populations, theses elaborated in Gunnar Heinsohn's *Söhne und Weltmacht* and endorsed by Sloterdijk (Therborn, 2009).

19 During the first decade of the new millennium, an anonymously authored column in the *Asia Times Online* provided a distinctive analysis of world politics. Written under the pen name 'Spengler', it criticised, among many other things, worldviews founded on the study of 'comparative social systems'. Against these – discernable in the writings of neoconservatives such as Fukuyama (1989), for whom the homogenising influence of the global market and liberal democracy heralded a future of boredom for the developed world – Huntington's emphasis on the religious foundations of each civilisation was singled out for praise (Spengler, 2009).

20 *Time*, 29 November 1943.

21 A tribute penned by French President François Mitterrand (1995), himself a *littérateur*, on the occasion of Jünger's hundredth birthday exemplifies the latter's straddling of aesthetic and political worlds.

22 A former Thatcherite like Ballard, Gray arrived gradually at this position over the course of the 1990s.

23 Fortuyn's death at the hands of an animal rights activist illustrates how, despite their shared aversions to modernity and European integration, the constellation of actors and movements examined in this chapter ought not to be thought of as a coherent group, their disparate orientations a catalyst to enmity. The murder of film-maker Theo van Gogh, a friend of Fortuyn's, by a radical Islamist also bears this out.

24   Indeed, as a former Marxist, Fortuyn's productivist orientation remained intact throughout his career, albeit in successively collectivist and individualist forms.

25   Christopher Caldwell (*Financial Times*, 26 November 2004), a second generation American neoconservative, has exhibited just such an analytical bias, reading Houellebecq's work as an indictment only of countercultural mores, rather than as a simultaneous judgement on consumerism and the market. More than Ballard (who resists the temptations of prudery), Houellebecq is ambivalent in this regard, juxtaposing sexual liberation and economic liberalism. Adorno's criticism of Aldous Huxley, acknowledged by Houellebecq as an influence, is apt: 'He fails to distinguish between the liberation of sexuality and its debasement' (Adorno, 1983: 103).

Caldwell's interpretation of Houellebecq is part of a broader misreading of Europe's orientations toward modernity, which are confused with those of America. For rather than, as he suggests, undergoing a puritanical disavowal of the 1960s, European antimodernism perpetuates itself, if Houellebecq and Fortuyn are anything to go by, through a commodification of that decade's excesses.

Though neglected by Caldwell and, earlier, Bell (Habermas, 1996a: 43), there are signs of increasing acknowledgement among neoconservatives of the normative consequences of advanced consumerism, particularly as it relates to the needs of the body. Reviewing a philosophical essay by Hervé Juvin, Perry Anderson (2006) draws attention to the disappointment with which it greets the triumph of capitalism: 'what communism set out to do, and disastrously failed to achieve, capitalism is in the process of realizing. The wildest of all the utopian revolutions gone is now taking shape before our eyes ... The arrival of a capitalism reduced to the ministrations of the body will be the ironic triumph of the most extravagant deliria of socialism' (Anderson, 2006: 136–8). The casualties of this process are the Protestant ethic and Western rationality; Hervé's tone is all the bleaker for the lack of a religious revivalism in Europe of the sort welcomed by Bell and his successors. A central plank of Juvin's thesis, and to some extent Houellebecq's (2001), is the uncoupling of the market from the spheres of ethics and ideology, and thus from the quest for self-mastery. This cognitive shift is, by contrast, greeted with enthusiasm by environmentalists Hawken, Lovins and Lovins: 'For all their power and vitality, markets are only tools. They make a good servant but a bad master and a worse religion' (1999: 261).

26   In an interview, Ratzinger said that if 'he were only able to take one book to a dessert island besides the Bible and Augustine's *Confessions* ... he would choose Hermann Hesse's Buddhist-inspired novella *Siddhartha*' (Shortt, 2010); reading of Ratzinger and Habermas's meeting, the author was reminded of Father Jacobus and Joseph Knecht's in Hesse's *The Glass Bead Game* (1943).

27   Dandyism is characteristic of continuum ii, encompassing subfeatures such as libertinism and camp. With reference to Jünger, George Steiner (1970: 14) employs the term 'in its strong, *condotierre* sense, as a comprehending asceticism and cool courage', referring back to the mercenary captains of the Renaissance who were frowned on by Machiavelli (1970: 77). Dandyism is often associated with decadent strains of Anglo-American and French literature. Though a detailed treatment is beyond the scope of the present study, the following writers – a far from comprehensive survey, to be sure – offer insights into the topic, whether as practitioners, theoreticians or observers: Lord Byron, Oscar Wilde, William Burroughs, J.G. Ballard, Chris Petit (specifically, the eponymous character from his novel *Robinson*, 1993), William Gibson (Peter Riviera, a protagonist in the latter's *Neuromancer*, 1984, is a classic, and rather sinister, dandy) and Susan Sontag, whose 'Notes on "Camp"' (1964) could be looked to for insights into the political style of, for example, Pim Fortuyn; among the French, obvious names are Sade, Baudelaire, Huysmans and

Houellebecq. Foucault was indebted to Baudelaire's conception of Dandyism (White, 1990: 146) – at an appropriately superficial level, his shaven head anticipated Fortuyn's (see also Jünger's, 1993: 31, sketch of Kessmüller).

How does this relate to the European project? As the rise of Fortuyn showed, the public mood in Europe during the Constitutional Convention was highly receptive to dandyism, contrasting strongly with that of the early postwar era, when, as Kaiser notes, enthusiasm reigned for

> a deliberately conservative, dull form of political representation and decision-making by 'indistinguishable "men in suits"' – the precise opposite of the flamboyant dictatorial style of the likes of Hitler and Mussolini. The more dull it was, the more reassuring. (Kaiser, 2007: 172)

On the left of the political spectrum, meanwhile, Leon Trotsky's sartorial tastes and reputation as a *littérateur* marked him out as a twentieth-century dandy. His example later influenced the Marxist counterculture of the 1960s, Christopher Hitchens remaining faithful to it even after his break from old comrades (Glazov, 2003); Blumenthal (2003: 606) has observed: 'As a political writer, Christopher Hitchens was a literary critic'.

PART III

Empirical research

8

The conceptual landscape of the Constitutional Convention

A critical social theory ought to provide a framework for empirical research, argues Habermas – it is not enough to inspire 'speculative observations' (Habermas, 1995: 382). With this in mind, the present chapter assesses data from a series of interviews conducted in 2002 against the background of the Constitutional Convention.[1] This is intended as a preliminary test of the accounts of social and cultural modernity elaborated thus far. Habermas's conception of the EU would be called into question if the observations of the interviewees diverged radically from it. Taken together, the responses assembled below bear out an idea of the EU as an incarnation of the siege model of democracy.

The attitudes of the left are examined first. A combination of centrists, social partners and institutional personnel then receives consideration.

The left

At different times, the radical and social democratic left[2] have been looked to by Habermas as *agents* of the reflective welfare state project, whether conceived of in national or postnational terms. In order to carry out this role, they would be expected to share a conception of the EU comparable with Habermas's own, particularly given the importance accorded by the left to theory as a guide to action. Yet the interviews considered below suggest that Habermas's engagement with the European project stemmed from a theoretical position too distinctive to inspire the left in its entirety (Grewal, 2001: 122). Indeed, the presence of a Eurosceptic tendency among the social democrats, coupled with the lukewarm, if not oppositional, attitude of the radical left, anticipated the French 'No' vote of 2005, where widespread opposition to the Bush administration's foreign policy failed to translate into support for the Constitution, as Habermas had hoped that it might (Habermas and Derrida, 2003: Habermas, 2005). In calling for intellectuals to play their part in constructing a European public sphere as the basis for a democratic Europe (Carleheden and Gabriëls, 1996: 16; Habermas and Derrida, 2003: 293), Habermas had shown an awareness of this 'conceptual deficit', though without rallying proselytizers and activists to his *theory* as, for example, Marx had sought to do.

A Swedish Left Party MEP eloquently summarised the attitudes of his peers, members of the EP's Group of the United European Left/Nordic Green Left (GUE-NGL), toward the EU:

> In my political group ... which is a far left mixture, I always tease them. I say, 'you are against economic policy, foreign policy, military policy, social policy, you are against all the policies, but you are for the Union – how come?' And then they don't know what to say, and then I say, 'its like in the good old days: we favoured a certain Union – though we hated its concrete policies, but somehow we thought the Union was good'.[3]

A combination of productivists and Greens, the GUE-NGL could be compared with the NSMs courted by Habermas in the 1980s. Those interviewed were critical of the EU, though the sorts of antimodernist sentiment identified by Habermas (1996a: 54) among sections of the German Green party were absent, more common perhaps in the rival Group of the Greens/European Free Alliance.

Members of the GUE-NGL were reluctant to detail a constructive programme for the EU's future. Their political horizons were delimited, not always consciously, by the nation-state. Indeed, a representative of the European Trade Union Confederation commented critically on their 'etatism'.[4] When a postnational praxis was broached at all, it recalled the insurrectionist variety theorised at around that time by Hardt and Negri (2000). One of those interviewed[5] did, however, claim to have grown more enthusiastic toward supranational governance since being elected. There was greater scope for such a learning process on the 'reformist' wing of the group, the Trotskyists retaining an attachment to Marxism–Leninism.

Reformists[6] envisaged the possibility that ideological conflict, particularly in relation to social policy, might one day be conducted at the European level. As yet, however, such concerns were seen through the lens of the nation-state, particularly the looming pensions crisis, which they thought soluble only through rises in domestic taxation.

No critique of productivism was forthcoming. When asked about this, a GUE-NGL representative[7] pointed to the unwillingness of Trotskyists even to consider the declining significance of organised labour, as postulated in Andre Gorz's *Farewell to the Working Class* (1980). A critical attitude toward the American social model was commonplace – however, only a minority saw the EU as the basis for an alternative.

GUE-NGL members lacked any sense of a *telos* to integration – whether in relation to the single market, the euro, or the Constitution; none conveyed a sense that the EU was following a juridification trajectory comparable with that of the nation-state, with a comprehensive welfare regime as its terminus. There was little faith, either, in the Charter of Fundamental Rights: arguing for the irrelevance of national constitutions, political struggle was presented as the only option.

Overall, there was less concern with national sovereignty than among other interviewees. The French Trotskyists,[8] for example, contrasted their abstention from the vote on the TEU with the 'No' campaigns mounted by the Communist Party and *Front National.*

Also heard was the call for welfare levels among poorer member states to be increased, even if harmonisation risked undermining the comparatively generous systems of Scandinavia. A Trotskyist[9] inclined toward this view, and it was commonplace among Scandinavians in the group,[10] in contrast to the defensive stances of a Swedish social democrat[11] and Danish independent[12] who also were interviewed. The hope expressed for a welfarist solidarity capable of uniting Swedes and Portuguese/Greeks was almost identical with Habermas's sentiments (1999a: 57). Though sceptical of market-administrative integration, the radical left echoed the idealism, emphasis on transnational solidarity and universalism of Habermas's political prescriptions.

What of the social democrats?

And good sense dictates ... the economy should bring progress to society, not the other way around.   —Delors, 1994[13]

MEPs and representatives of the Party of European Socialists (PES), along with the trade unionists interviewed,[14] had quite different views to those of the radical left. These social democrats exceeded even Habermas in their hopes for the Constitution, euro, ESM and Charter of Fundamental Rights. The latter were looked to as sources of legitimacy for the European project, and – recalling Parsonian systems theory and neofunctionalism – portrayed in quite deterministic terms as preconditions for a European welfare regime. At the same time, calls for democratic participation were less common than among members of the GUE-NGL; when 'politicisation'[15] or a 'political Europe'[16] were mentioned at all, the tone was traditionally social democratic and productivist. Nevertheless, there was concern at the present condition of social Europe: as in Leibfried's work (2005; Leibfried and Pierson, 2000), this centred on the inadequacy of EU social policy as a response to the erosion of the welfare state.

Taken *together* the GUE-NGL and PES echoed Habermas's political prescriptions. In itself, however, each group held only to a portion of these. The differing viewpoints recalled somewhat the 'internal' and 'external' perspectives of the lifeworld and system.

A second social democratic tendency, sceptical toward European integration and defensive in relation to the welfare state, was also in evidence, hailing in particular from the Scandinavian and Anglo-Saxon peripheries.[17] An English economist of the DG for Employment and Social Affairs[18] adopted a line of argument common among right-wing social democrats after 9/11 (see

Goodhart, 2004), stating that migratory flows were inimical to social cohesion.

Centrists, social partners and institutional personnel

With the exception of staff from the Council Legal Service (CLS), the centrists, social partners and institutional personnel[19] who were interviewed also conveyed an impression of the EU evocative of the siege model. Perceptions of the democratic deficit varied.

In relation to Social Europe, something like Leibfried and Pierson's (1995abc, 2000) moderate neofunctionalist model was commonly attested to. However, opinions differed along left/right lines as to the seriousness and implications of the 'welfare gap', with trade unionists placing particular emphasis on the problem. There was little sense of there yet being a European public sphere, though, in contrast to the left, concern at this state of affairs was minimal.

Overall, there was only a vague sense of European integration as a *political* project, interviewees perceiving it largely through the 'conceptual lenses' (Cram, 1997: 2) of institutional affiliation. None saw Fortuyn's rise to prominence as a consequence of the integration process, despite its unsettling coincidence with the Constitutional Convention.

Christian Democrats shared the attachment of those on the centre left to the Constitution and ESM; without the latter, it was argued, the Single Market would not have been acceptable to electorates in the first place. However, the democratic deficit[20] and welfare gap[21] were not seen as serious problems. Indeed, in contrast to the trade unionists,[22] Christian Democrats felt that a developed structure of social dialogue was already in place at the European level. EU social policy was not foreseen by Christian Democrats as the subject of transnational conflicts between left and right, though one of them did concede that tensions might arise between national welfare cultures.[23]

A Liberal Democrat from the UK[24] argued that the ESM was inseparable from the fabric of its constituent national cultures. As such, and on the grounds of subsidiarity, it ought not to be a concern of EU policy making. Civil rights and the Common Foreign and Security Policy, were, by contrast, seen as legitimate areas for supranational governance.

A representative of the European People's Party (EPP-ED) expressed views closer to the 'Market European' perspective, questioning the very feasibility of the Charter of Fundamental Rights. A significant (and beneficial) level of negative welfare state harmonisation was, however, seen to have come about through the free movement of workers. Among other things, this process had effected a greater commodification of healthcare, due simply to the imperative that patients receive equivalent levels of treatment across the EU.[25]

There was consensus among representatives of the Union of Employers and Industrial Confederations of Europe (UNICE),[26] European Bureau of Consumer Unions (BEUC),[27] European Trade Union Confederation (ETUC)[28] and English trade unionists:[29] all spoke of a steady increase in social dialogue at the European level. The ETUC, however, sought more, criticising UNICE's refusal to include wage bargaining as a topic of discussion. All exhibited a productivist frame of reference; UNICE was credited by its representative with having no interest in the ESM (or, indeed, the European project) beyond that relevant to its immediate strategic interests.

In common with the Europhile social democrats, the trade unionists were generally enthusiastic toward the Constitution, euro and ESM. Representatives of the General, Municipal, Boilermakers and Allied Trade Union (GMB) also spoke of a systematic reorientation of responsibilities to their office in Brussels, a classic case of neofunctionalist spillover.[30] German trade unionists[31] were especially positive toward the Constitution, one of them[32] – echoing a constitution specialist from the German foreign ministry[33] and a German representative[34] of the Committee of Permanent Representatives (COREPER) – citing parallels between it and the German Basic Law, a theme of Habermas's writings. The trade unionists also emphasised the differences between the European and American social models, expressing a preference for the former. Those from the UK[35] spoke of a 'backlash' against the ESM, charging the British government with dragging its feet on the implementation of social regulations.

The Economic and Social Committee (ESC) was formed to give civil society a consultative voice in the EC policy-making process. It comprises three groups: those of Employers, Workers and Various Interests. Those who were interviewed matched the social partners in their support for the Constitution, yet their involvement in long-term, largely technical, deliberation, tended to promote more harmonious working relationships than those of the latter – members expressed pride at the 'Platonic' attitudes characteristic of their deliberations. Nevertheless, those in the Various Interests group claimed that without their mediation disputes between the Employers and Workers would have been more difficult to resolve. Other interviewees thought the ESC an ineffectual organisation, its heyday the Delors era. A former social policy specialist for Delors' think tank, *Notre Europe*, went further, arguing in relation to social policy that influence had waned not only for the ESC, but for the social partners and Commission as well.[36]

The COREPER employees who were approached all stated that their primary aim was the maximisation of national autonomy in their field of specialisation, employment and social policy. The British,[37] French,[38] German[39] and Swedish[40] analysts also explained that the EU's influence in this sphere had grown beyond the predictions of state-centrists to exert a significant influence on domestic arenas. This was perceived with enthusiasm by the German interviewee, in common with a constitution specialist from the German foreign ministry. The former also argued that changes of government in the Council of Ministers had little impact on national preferences of this sort. His French counterpart, by contrast, favoured subsidiarity as a way of insulating his country's welfare regime from potential incursions by the EU. The tone of other COREPER staff was even more defensive. The Swedish interviewee considered even the most technical pieces of legislation in terms of their likely impacts on domestic public opinion. The British interviewee, meanwhile, echoed a Green Party MEP and compatriot with the claim that EU social policy was itself a source of the democratic deficit, particularly due to the influence of the social partners' deliberations.

Alone among those interviewed, staff from the CLS strongly disputed a systems-theoretic conception of EU social policy, whether evocative of Leibfried's work or Majone's. Instead, one of them defended the intergovernmentalist perspective,[41] while two others[42] emphasised the importance of the ECJ, recalling the legal contextualism of scholars such as Caporaso (2000) and Shaw (2001). The intergovernmentalist attested to a widespread, if basic, familiarity with BFN on the part of lawyers employed by EU institutions, though he went on to state that Constitutional Patriotism had little, if any, relevance beyond the nation-state. The democratic deficit was played down by the staff of the CLS, and there was faith that the EU would continue to derive output legitimacy from the execution of legal and technocratic functions.

Staff of the Directorate General (DG) for Employment and Social Affairs[43] put forward a variety of views; even in relation to economic and social policy, there was little uniformity of opinion. Nevertheless, there was optimism toward the Constitution, which, it was believed, would endow the EU with greater legitimacy. There was also a modicum of consensus on the unexceptional achievements and likely prospects of EU social policy, though only one interviewee[44] endorsed the welfare gap thesis in its entirety. A trade unionist[45] with links to this DG claimed that its initiatives were frequently opposed, and even thwarted, by the DG for Competition, a testament to the Commission's collegiate, even somewhat 'Balkanised', structure (Ross, 1995).

Notes

1 The interviews referred to in this chapter were conducted by the author in Berlin, Brussels, Paris and the UK in 2002. In each case, a set of open questions – relating to EU social policy, democratic legitimacy, European identity and prescriptions for reform – provided the basis for discussion.

2 The radical left: GUE-NGL Political Group Secretariat employee (Employment and Social Affairs), 18 October 2002; Swedish Left Party MEP, 2 October 2002; Portuguese Communist MEP, 8 October 2002; UK Green MEP, 31 May 2002; French Trotskyist MEP, 11 October 2002; GUE-NGL Political Group Secretariat employee (Employment and Social Affairs), 9 October 2002; Danish Independent (June Movement) MEP, 2 October 2002 (though not ideologically of the radial left, the

author categorised this interviewee alongside the latter on the grounds of her vigorous defence, in the face of European integration, of the Danish social model and social partners arrangements).

The social democratic left: PES Political Group Secretariat employee (Employment and Social Affairs), 17 September 2002; PES Political Group Secretariat employee (Trade), 3 October 2002; PES Political Group Secretariat employee (Employment and Social Affairs), 11 October 2002; UK Labour MEP, 17 May 2002; Swedish Social Democrat MEP, 19 October 2002.

3   Interview with a Swedish Left Party MEP, 2 October 2002.
4   Interview with an ETUC/ETUI representative, 7 October 2002.
5   Interview with a Scandinavian GUE-NGL Political Group Secretariat employee (Employment and Social Affairs), 18 October 2002.
6   Interview with a Scandinavian GUE-NGL Political Group Secretariat employee (Employment and Social Affairs), 18 October 2002, and a UK Green MEP, 31 May 2002.
7   Private conversation with a German GUE-NGL Political Group Secretariat employee (Employment and Social Affairs), 9 October 2002.
8   Interview with a French Trotskyist MEP (*Lutte Ouvrière*) and a party colleague, 11 October 2002.
9   Interview with a French Trotskyist MEP (*Lutte Ouvrière*) and a party colleague, 11 October 2002.
10 Interviews with a Swedish Left Party MEP, 2 October 2002, and a Scandinavian GUE-NGL Political Group Secretariat employee (Employment and Social Affairs), 18 October 2002.
11 Interview with a Swedish Social Democrat MEP, 19 October 2002.
12 Interview with a Danish independent (June Movement) MEP, 2 October 2002.
13 Jacques Delors cited in Geyer, 2000: 203.
14 Interview with an ETUC/ETUI representative, 7 October 2002. Interview with a representative of the EMCEF trade union, 18 September 2002. Interviews with a National Secretary of the GMB, 16 October 2002, and the European Officer of the GMB, 16 October 2002.
15 Interview with a UK Labour MEP, 17 May 2002.
16 Interview with a PES Political Group Secretariat employee (Employment and Social Affairs), 17 September 2002.
17 Interviews with a Swedish Social Democrat MEP, 19 October 2002, and a Danish independent (June Movement) MEP, 2 October 2002.
18 Interview with an English economist from the DG Employment and Social Affairs, 30 September 2002.
19 Centrists: Luxembourg Christian Democrat MEP, 8 October 2002; Dutch Christian Democrat MEP, 19 September 2002; UK Liberal Democrat MEP, 2 October 2002; EPP-ED Political Group Secretariat employee, 10 October 2002.

Social partners: Representative of the ETUC/ETUI, 7 October 2002; Representative of EMCEF, 18 September 2002; National Secretary of the GMB, 16 October 2002; European Officer of the GMB, 16 October 2002; Social Affairs Adviser UNICE, 4 October 2002; Representative of BEUC, 23 September 2002; Specialist from FEANTSA, 25 September 2002; Specialist from FEANTSA, 23 September 2002; International Secretary (1993-1999) of the EUW, 12 June 2002.

Institutional personnel: Scholar from DG Research, 3 October 2002; Constitutional Specialist from the German Foreign Ministry, 23 July 2002; German COREPER specialist in social policy, 10 October 2002; French COREPER specialist in social policy, 4 October, 2002; UK COREPER specialist in social policy, 17 October 2002; Swedish COREPER specialist in social policy, 24 October 2002; Head of Social

Protection and Inclusion from DG Employment and Social Affairs, 17 September 2002; Specialist from DG Employment and Social Affairs, 19 September, 2002; Economist at DG Employment and Social Affairs, 30 September 2002; Representative of the Council Legal Service, 26 September 2002; Representative of the Council Legal Service, 14 October; Representative of the Council Legal Service, 27 September 2002; Specialist on relations between domestic and European parliaments, 19 September 2002; ESC Secretariat General employee (Directorate B – Social and Citizenship), 1 October 2002; ESC – (French) Employers (Section for EMU and Economic and Social Cohesion), 17 June 2002; ESC – (French) Labour, 16 October 2002; ESC – (French) Various Interests, 18 September 2002; ESC (and CEPLIS) – (French) Various Interests, 26 September 2002; Head of Research at 'Policy Network' (formerly the social policy specialist at *Notre Europe*, Delors' think tank), 27 June 2002.

20   Interview with a Christian Democrat MEP from Luxembourg, 8 October 2002.

21   Interview with a Christian Democrat MEP from Holland, 19 September 2002.

22   Interview with an ETUC/ETUI representative, 7 October 2002. Interview with a representative of the EMCEF trade union, 18 September 2002. Interviews with a National Secretary of the GMB, 16 October 2002, and the European Officer of the GMB, 16 October 2002.

23   Interview with a Christian Democrat MEP from Holland, 19 September 2002.

24   Interview with a UK Liberal Democrat MEP, 2 October 2002.

25   Interview with an employee of the Political Group Secretariat of the EPP-ED, 10 October 2002.

26   Interview with a UNICE representative, 4 October 2002.

27   Interview with a BEUC representative, 23 October 2002.

28   Interview with an ETUC/ETUI representative, 7 October 2002.

29   Interviews with the National Secretary and European Officer of the GMB, 16 October 2002.

30   Interviews with the National Secretary and European Officer of the GMB, 16 October 2002.

31   Interview with an ETUC/ETUI representative, 7 October 2002. Interview with a representative of the EMCEF trade union, 18 September 2002.

32   Interview with an ETUC/ETUI representative, 7 October 2002.

33   Interview with a Constitutional Specialist from the German Foreign Ministry, 23 July 2002.

34   Interview with a German COREPER specialist in social policy, 10 October 2002.

35   Interview with the European Officer of the GMB, 16 October 2002.

36   Interview with the Head of Research at Policy Network (formerly the social policy specialist at *Notre Europe*, Delors' think tank), 27 June 2002.

37   Interview with a UK social policy representative of COREPER, 17 October 2002.

38   Interview with a French social policy representative of COREPER, 4 October 2002.

39   Interview with a German social policy representative of COREPER, 10 October 2002.

40   Interview with a Swedish social policy representative of COREPER, 24 October 2002.

41   Interview with a representative of the Council Legal Service, 14 October 2002.

42   Interviews with representatives of the Council Legal Service, 26 and 27 September 2002.

43   Interviews with Head of Social Protection and Inclusion from DG Employment and Social Affairs, 17 September 2002; Specialist from DG Employment and Social Affairs, 19 September, 2002; and an Economist at DG Employment and Social Affairs, 30 September 2002.

44   Interview with Head of Social Protection and Inclusion from DG Employment and Social Affairs, 17 September 2002.

45   Interview with the European Officer of the GMB, 16 October 2002.

Conclusion
An unfinished project?

> In Djerzinski's time, philosophy was generally considered to be of no practical significance, to have been stripped of its purpose. Nevertheless, the values to which a majority subscribe at any given time determine society's economic and political structures and social mores.
>
> Metaphysical mutations – that is to say radical, global transformations in the values to which the majority subscribe – are rare in the history of humanity. The rise of Christianity might be cited as an example.
>
> Once a metaphysical mutation has arisen, it tends to move inexorably towards its logical conclusion. Heedlessly, it sweeps away economic and political systems, ethical considerations and social structures. No human agency can halt its progress – nothing, but another metaphysical mutation.—Houellebecq, 1998[1]

> There are no riots, no extremists in power, no abrogation of civil liberties, no postponement of elections. Still, I think there is a crisis in Europe. It is a crisis in minds rather than on the streets – and disorder in the mind, in our ideas and loyalties, can be even more dangerous than its more visible counterparts.
> —Siedentop, 2005[2]

A novel conception of the EU has informed Habermas's political prescriptions. For this conception to be delineated accurately, two bodies of work must be reckoned with: Habermas's scholarly writings and political journalism. This chapter casts a glance in both directions.

The preceding accounts of social and cultural modernity are considered first; promising avenues for research are suggested. Attention then turns to the political context that Habermas addressed. The failure of the Constitutional project and, five years on, the crisis of the eurozone can be traced to the same underlying 'conceptual deficit': a dearth of postnational political thought. A reluctance to transcend the nation-state as a frame of reference has characterised elites as well as European populations – only a minority of key players (the late Tommaso Padoa-Schioppa[3], for example) have stated this to be a problem.

A critical theory of European integration

Social modernity at the level of the EU was the theme of chapters 1 to 4, a survey of Habermas's political journalism guiding the theoretical reflections that followed. Two lines of inquiry were suggested. The first was metatheoretical: reflection on the *condominio* trajectory of juridification, with its ontology of system-lifeworld dialectic, was intended to stimulate discussion of the EU's fundamental nature and purpose. John Goff's afterword takes steps in that direction. While critical of specifics, he acknowledges the importance of Habermas's postnational turn, suggesting lines along which philosophical discussions of the EU and globalisation might be conducted in future.

At a lower level of abstraction, social modernity can be examined in relation to specific historical conjunctures or policy contexts. With reference to the former, this study has centred on the era of the Constitutional Convention, which, for example, frames the discussion of the *Lijst Pim Fortuyn* undertaken in chapter four. The issues of privacy and information security that are also broached in that chapter call urgently for empirical research.

The treatment of cultural modernity undertaken in chapters five to seven might inspire quite general questions – for example, whether Europessimism is but a subset of the broader cultural pessimism that has assailed the project of modernity in recent decades – or be approached with more specific research goals in mind. An instance of the latter would be the utilisation of the Eurosceptic categories of chapter seven – 'deep', 'folk', 'mainstream' and 'populist' – alongside the discourse oriented approach of Trenz and de Wilde (2009).

Recent political theory confronts scholars of European integration with difficult questions. Among the most pressing of these is posed by McCormick:

> It is only after the most careful study that the following possibility can be confronted with the requisite perspective, maturity, and gravity: that the age of legally secured democratic government is over, and that the transition to a globalized age is even more of a drastic historical-structural rupture than was the transition from the *Rechtsstaat* to the *Sozialstaat*. Only then can we ponder whether the earlier transformation at least allowed for some continuity of and adaptation for principles and practices of self-government, political and economic liberty, socioeconomic equality, elite accountability, and so on, while the latest structural transformation of the state, quite simply, does not. (McCormick, 2007: 289)

In the course of a meticulous argument, McCormick casts doubt on the contributions that either TCA or BFN could make to answering this question. This study is intended to demonstrate their continuing relevance.

A (post)metaphysical mutation

Habermas's campaigning in favour of the European Constitution would seem vindicated by the crisis of the eurozone; certainly, the case for fiscal harmonisation – a precondition for the long-term stability of the euro (Münchau, 2010), and perhaps for the EU's survival – would have had a more favourable political context had citizens across the continent endorsed a constitutional order. Ultimately, Habermas's conception of the EU was too narrowly disseminated to influence either elite or popular opinion. This study is intended, in a small way, to address that state of affairs, though it is not to be suggested that theories, even as brilliant his, will provide easy answers to Europe's complex problems.

In the era of the Constitutional Convention, antimodernists such as Houellebecq seemed to explain the popular mood in Europe. It is a testament to the richness and sophistication of Habermas's ideas that they supported, and continue to still, an alternative – postmetaphysical – interpretation.

Notes

1   Houellebecq (2001a: 4).
2   Siedentop (2005: 26).
3   See Padoa-Schioppa (2010).

Afterword

John Goff

When the question of European integration is posed, it immediately evokes the question of its purpose. What is such integration for? And this immediately brings forward another two questions: what is the European Union for, and what, fundamentally, *is* the European Union?

If the question of European integration is both a political and an emotional question, a matter not only of power but also of lifeworld *feeling*, then these two further questions, of its purpose and mode of being, are at once metaphysical and practical political questions.

In distinction to the *activity* of the European Union in political-economic and social-cultural domains, there is also the significant matter of how to *think about* the European Union. This further question, about the ways in which the European Union might be thought or conceptualised, evokes something like a *philosophy of* the European Union. And a further question as to whether the development of a *philosophical* understanding of the European Union is a worthwhile endeavour.

In recent years, it seems that serious philosophical examination of the European Union has been relatively scarce. Jürgen Habermas is significant in this regard because he has developed a philosophy of the European Union, in part. However, this philosophy has not been rendered explicit. Shivdeep Grewal has done significant work here to make not only Habermas's philosophy of the European Union explicit, but in so doing to begin to ground philosophy of the European Union as a viable domain of intellectual effort and concern.

There are thus two key moments in Shivdeep Grewal's study: one, to treat the European Union as an object of philosophical, intellectual interest as such and two, to use Habermas's thought as the instrument for rendering visible the contours of such a study. One may then, on the one hand, put the European Union and Habermas together in a harmony of kinds but also, on the other hand, apart in tension – one does not have to follow Habermas's philosophical take on the European Union to acknowledge its importance. It seems then that Shivdeep Grewal also works with these harmonious and tense aspects to show where one might follow Habermas and where not by revealing the relevance of his idea of *modernity* in this area of concern.

In practice, this involves asking about the activity of the European Union relative to the 'unfinished project of modernity' and whether this activity is of a form sufficient to finish the project of modernity in the sense of bringing it to completion. In order to attempt to answer this question – and further to decide whether European integration furthers the project of modernity or not – one must attempt also to answer the prior questions as to the 'purpose' and mode of 'being' (or 'nature') of the European Union.

EU: 'end' or 'means'?

Some leverage on the question of what the European Union *is* may be obtained by drawing a distinction between ends and means. Is the EU an end or a means? If this question could be decided, then this would go some way towards answering the question as to what the EU is *for*, and whether integration is required to fulfil its purpose.

Why might these questions be posed again? Surely, they were answered in the process of founding the European Economic Community (EEC) and then the EU? It is here that the travails of 'modernity' enter the picture. If it is proposed that the development of the EEC was consonant with the overall goals of modernity, it may also be proposed that as 'modernity' as such fell into question, so, by implication, did the liaison of modernity and the integration of a European Community – to the point that the EU has become not much more than the ongoing functioning of its institutions within their own terms of reference. The eurosceptic critique is that the EU appears to be little more than these institutional activities undertaken for their own sake – it is closed in its own self-reference and is functioning contrary to the geopolitical realpolitik. To attempt to answer what the EU is, or has become, is to pose, once more, a political-metaphysical question about means and ends.

In the period following World War II, and given the geopolitical position of Western Europe in the Cold War era, the EEC made sense not only as an economic means but also as a political axis consequent on European economic development and Western security interests. The fall of the Berlin Wall and the increased momentum of globalisation suddenly shifted the practical political-economic context within which the European political-economic community attempted to define itself. As it stands, at the time of writing, the question of whether further European integration serves to further the development of efficient political-economic means in the emerging era of globality is a pressing, and much disputed, question. And also whether globality as such – however it is characterised – continues or variously dissipates the project of 'modernity'.

Questions of purpose (teleology) and mode of being (ontology), subsequent to the questions of integration and modernity, once more are not simply philosophical but deeply practical questions. In the light of the critique of modernity, the work that Shivdeep Grewal, following Habermas, puts into an analysis of conservatism as 'contra-modernity' is timely. Diverse 'contra-modernists' will tend towards either a dissipation of the EU in favour of enhanced forms of nation-statism, or else towards the EU as a defence against globalisation. The EU is at the centre of a series of complex political-economic and social-cultural tensions that require working through. The tangled tensions and harmonies of the 'system-lifeworld' complex must be brought into philosophical consciousness since they form the knots out of which political will is projected. However, before an answer attempted at the questions of integration and modernity may be addressed, what then of those of purpose and ontology?

Is the EU a means or an end? Of course, such a question is difficult to answer, and requires a subtle separation of the philosophical/metaphysical from the political, but one might begin by asking: if the EU were an end, what sort of end might this be? It is here that one might draw on Aristotle's concept of final cause but differentiate it between external and internal purposes and functions – in other words between what something is for (purpose) and what it does (function).

What the EU, officially, *does* (its function) is to progressively enable a single market for the benefit of its members (whether it functions well or badly in doing this is a question outside the scope of this afterword). The achievement of this function involves, of course, a whole complex of other functions. In so far as it does this, one might argue that the purpose of the EU is achieved as and when this single market functions as it ought to. By these lights, the EU has as its overall end an efficient and beneficial economy.

If one accepts that this is the only end of the EU, then evaluation of the EU may be achieved in so far as one has common criteria for measuring economic success. However, very clearly this does not exhaust either the functioning or the purpose of the EU since bringing about a single market is not simply a matter of efficient economic management but is a deeply political process involving, as it does, nation-states trading off parts of their sovereignty for projected overall economic benefits. The EU is political, and the achievement of a single market is a project with complex historical and political implications and effects. Not least, in so far as this market is either a single one or singular among markets in the world; nor, in so far as it answers the question of the relative priority of the economic in human affairs. This latter, a complex question posed by Hannah Arendt in her *The Human Condition* (1958) and one which may be posed back at the EU: are we building just an efficient and productive economy or something *much more* which that single market enables? Eurosceptics have long since claimed that the economic purpose has been overtaken by a political purpose, but arguments remain as to what this political purpose is.

In attempting to discern a purpose, and in distinguishing purpose from function, one might propose several *external* political purposes such as the development of European 'soft power' and 'influence', the defence of a

European 'way of life', the promotion of forms of 'global governance' and so on. Furthermore, one might suggest more hidden, even 'dark' and 'involuted', purposes such as the negotiation of a European post-colonial consciousness and the consequent projection of a virtual/cultural empire grounded in claims to a specifically European world understanding. Indeed, the specification of external purposes is a central part of European policy making. The absence of such specification of purpose leading to a sense of drift and stagnation, supposedly to be solved by the EU speaking in 'one voice'. The problem being, of course, that of *whose* voice – that of a choir? The patterns of EU enunciation and vocalisation in themselves contain a politics.

But what about 'internal' purpose? Drawing on Aristotle's final cause, such internal purpose is achieved when an agent or organism most fully expresses its own nature and achieves the expression of its 'essence' to the fullest degree. But such a question immediately calls on the ontological question: what *is* the EU? Is the EU an end-in-itself, a final cause in flourishing? Can the EU be an end-in-itself? The answer to this question depends on whether one thinks the EU is something for which a final cause (flourishing) arises.

It is relatively easy to say what the EU is in definition: a political-economic alliance holding several key institutions and functions in common (through law). In such a bare definition, the alliance members are posited as having persistent, enduring existence. However, this only begs further questions as to the ontology of these members: are nation-states not also alliances, and is the definition not thus recursive? A general question as to the ontology of alliance still persists, then – one has to say what an alliance *is*. Does one then call on systems, network and organisation theories, and begin to ask questions about the ontologies of systems, networks and organisations? Such an exercise in (what amounts to) mereology might appear empty – or too rather generally philosophical – were it not for the political consequences of deciding on such ontologies. The EU has been brought into *existence* but has it been brought into persistence, purpose and power? If so, in virtue of what? If, however, it has not persistence, purpose and power then is it simply a means for those of its members that do? The question of integration poses these questions of *political* ontology by posing questions as to the locus of power.

EU ontology: 'system' or 'network'?

The question of integration further poses that of unity. Is there any sense in which the EU – further integrated – might form a unity? Might one then count it as 1? But in what sense a unity? In what then might such unity lie? How might such unity be effected? In law? In the familiar terrain of a constitution? Or perhaps, also, in drawing a boundary and a distinction between EU and not EU? Might one then understand Habermas's 'constitutionalism' – and 'constitutional patriotism' – as a claim on the EU as a unity in the sense of something that realises an enlightened constitution that binds its constituents in an ethical-legal world that is also its end? Following an extractive method, if one takes law (juridification) away is one still left with the EU? If one takes boundaries away, is one still left with the EU? Furthermore, might one argue that the EU is not given in a singular ontology, but rather in several ontologies? Where does this get one? Well quite some way, because it means that one may begin to conceptualise the EU not as something singular and unitary – despite the appearance of its institutions and its name – but rather as a set of overlapping ontologies and their diverse processes. Such a conceptualisation becomes important when one wants to think of the EU as an 'agent' effecting something like a *will* when in negotiation. However, if there is no EU as such, then there are, at best, a series of wills or actions grounded only in its members. An alliance then, yes, but one given in tension, perhaps, rather than harmony. An alliance bound *by* a constitution rather than *through* one (the difference between the EU and American constitutions?).

Despite the outward appearance of law as a binding force, if one distinguishes between the concepts of system, network and organisation, then one might (by stipulation) propose that whereas both systems and networks are organised, systems are organised as *unities* whereas networks are *non-unitary*. This amounts to saying something like that systems admit of organisational completion, whereas networks do not. A system admits of wholeness in the sense of the whole being more than the sum of its parts, whereas a network is non-holistic and is simply a pattern (or set of patterns) of organised parts. A system may thus persist in finality, a network persists only in liaison. Such (stipulated) conceptual distinction-making amounts to asking whether, ontologically, the EU is a system or a network. Something organised as a unity and a whole or not, something that may persist in finality or otherwise only in liaison.

Deciding whether the EU is a system or a network (in the use of terms just given) will go a long way to deciding whether it has an end and whether that end is internal or external (for the sake of brevity, further componential or fractional analysis of the EU along these lines will not be pursued, here). This will also assist in deciding whether, overall, the EU is a means for its members or an end-in-itself.

Clearly, the EU is organised via law and is given in the set of institutions that function as its organisational means. However, in terms of our more abstract consideration of organisational ontology, this does not tell us much about whether to consider the EU as a system or as a network. One may then just model the EU as either a system or as a network and then consider what intellectual leverage such consideration provides.

If a key property of a system is its wholeness, in that the whole is more than the sum of its parts (a system admits of existence beyond that of its component members), as a whole, it is able to define itself further by a boundary. Systems are also architectonic, structured in part-whole relations at several levels. The most obvious entities that fit this description are biological/animal ones, where an architecture of cells, organs and anatomical parts are arranged to produce a creature that is more than the sum of its parts – we may speak of the creature but not as just its parts, of which we must speak separately. Furthermore, a system admits of reflexivity in so far as it may act upon itself from higher to lower levels. A system has an end even if this is only a form of self-preservation which may be given in its reflexive preservation of boundary. In this, systems admit of cognitive functions and intelligent action – very evident in systems such as animals, but more problematic when extended beyond the biological. The key question concerning whether some pattern of organisation is a system or not is whether it constitutes a unity or not. This ontological question – is the EU a system or not? – is at once a political question. If it is a system, then it has an architecture given in part-whole relations, reflexivity, an end through which its unity is constituted and which its unity constitutes, and holism in so far as it is greater than the sum of its parts.

If one thinks that it may be hard either to model the EU as a system by these lights, or that only biological entities might count as systems, might one do better then to model the EU, non-holistically, as a dynamic network with diverse nodes of influence and control but without any unity? If it is the case that one is better off to think like this, then such a model will not be unique to the EU. However, the problems posed by such a way of thinking may be more forceful in thinking of the EU. In other words, that such thoughts come to the fore and insist on consideration in the case of the EU. By and large, the question of unity in the case of nation-states only tends to be problematic in times of crisis (it may be a common, if erroneous, assumption that nation-states are systems) – but for the EU it is a problematic given in the very process of construction and understanding. One may then wish to begin to think of the EU not as a unity – despite the legalistic framework – but rather as a set of network configurations traversing political-economic and social-cultural domains. In that case, the EU subsists given its momentum and dissipates as the complex of political-economic and social-cultural threads that hold 'it' together begin to interweave with diverse other threads beyond its legal/institutional boundaries. If the EU actually involves the construction of a network, it may be the construction of a network of means and functions identified via a set of institutions but not immanent in them. EU membership entails not much more than a set of permissions to access this network.

As a network, the EU may have no internal purpose because it has no ontology as a system, it is not a unity nor a whole, but rather a name for a sequence of liaisons and a certain political-economic momentum. One might propose that rather than an organisation, the EU is an *organising* – further emphasising the shift from an architectonic, systemic understanding to a dynamic, relational one.

Further to these considerations, one might pose the question: might the EU be an end in itself in virtue of an *idea* that it realises? This is the *dream* of constitutionalism. Perhaps, one moves closer to a Platonic conception here and further from the more 'Aristotelian' approaches discussed previously. The EU might be constructed and maintained because its idea, and idealisation, is worthwhile achieving in and of itself. Simply, the EU is good and worthwhile in itself because it achieves an idea. But what might such an idea be? One proposal – and one presumes close to that of Habermas – is the completion of the project of modernity in the form of an enlightened *social* modernity. The EU may be an end in itself in so far as it achieves a specific form (idea) of modernity such that the European lifeworld is transformed. In other words, modernity is completed in its full unfolding. Might the EU not only be the means for but also the realisation of this complete unfolding of modernity? Here then conceptions of modernity are raised to consideration, but the relevant conception here would be that of 'enlightenment' shorn of its pure instrumentality – the critical object of the Frankfurt School – and dialectically unfolded under communicative reason.

EU, Modernity and Globality

For Habermas, modernity is completed in the emergence of a stable ethico-legal society that at once achieves the goals of economic development but also brings into existence a version of Kant's 'perpetual peace' whilst subsuming techno-scientific rationality towards moral and aesthetic ends. To this end – Habermas's version of Aristotelian flourishing? – the EU must be, at least, a means through its Social Model, and processes of juridification, but surely also an exemplar (Platonic idea, form). But what does this exemplar exemplify? Something like a *republic of reason* – an enlightened political and public state of affairs shorn of instrumentalism? The end of the EU lies in its promotion of various registers of normative, completed 'Habermasian' modernity. The EU is to define itself by an idea rather than a boundary, but in practice that boundary is set against those that fall foul its idea. Its realpolitik is the prosecution of an exemplified modernity of perpetual peace. It is to this end that European integration and the binding of the nation-state in a wider constitutionalism is required. The EU is the first post-national *unity* in so far as it realises a completed *social* modernity. The nation-state is insufficiently modern – that is, not fully unfolded – because it is insufficiently universal. Indeed, the nation-state takes its legitimacy from its historical lifeworld, and lifeworld imperatives may fall foul of enlightened norms. Without the transformation of the lifeworld – in so far as it is shorn of contra-modern tendencies – there cannot be the completion of modernity. Modernity must thus transform forms of life in the direction of a modern human flourishing – tradition may play little part in this process. The EU in transforming the lifeworlds of its constituents undermines the basis of legitimacy for the nation-state. The nation-state legitimises system (bureaucratic, techno-scientific, instrumental) imperatives through a rhetoric of the lifeworld, which may yet express a range of 'unwholesome' atavisms.

The question of modernity may be continued relative to the question of globality. If one takes globality to be that condition of the world which is realised through globalisation, then a question arises as to whether globality continues the trajectory of modernity or not. If not, then if one takes a 'Habermasian' EU as being one in which the project of modernity is completed there will be a tense relation between the EU, as the realisation of the idea of modernity, and globality as something other than modernity. Will the political role of the EU then be to transform globality into realised modernity? However, if globality is not the realisation of modernity, then what is it? Here, globalisation (in distinction to globality) may be understood to follow in the trajectory of modernity in so far as it is the realisation of developmental goals but, primarily, through the instrumental imperatives of the state-market complex. However, the trajectory of modernity brings about not only lifeworld turbulence but also the techno-scientific transformation of the lifeworld in directions that may not be consonant with the enlightened ideals of a completed modernity. The manner in which technological transformation stimulates or augments a complex of libidinal-aggressive tendencies has been much expressed in Ballard's work (as referenced by Shivdeep Grewal) but also has been the basis for the dystopian visions of writers such as William Gibson and a range of cyberpunks and cyber-libertarians. In short, the transformative power of globalisation through techno-science may be such as to undermine a European 'republic of reason' and dissipate any ethico-legal, aesthetic consensus. Globality may be such that it is both creative, constructive and dissipative, destructive in diverse proportions but not amenable to ethico-legalistic framing and control. Indeed, globality may be just a dynamic condition, and something for which an *end* (or purpose) does not arise – the very spontaneity of its order undermining anything like a rational plan. We cope with globality rather than control or design it.

In such a scenario, a Habermasian EU will be one which is engaged in an ongoing task of trying to bring a modern order to a global, dynamic spontaneity. To this end, the integration of the EU is defined relative to globality and not to the nation-state. Indeed, part of the EU and nation-state problematic may lie in the attractiveness of a spontaneous, libidinal-aggressive lifeworld to a great many 'conservatives' (contra-moderns) whether in the visage of liberty (young conservatives) or, on the contrary, in the attempt to stem these libidinal-aggressive tendencies via national traditions, but also against what is perceived as the cold rationality of modernity (old conservatives).

Only in so far as a realised social modernity is also able to manage our libidinal-aggressive tendencies will it be able to offset the destructive or dissipative effects of these. In short, a Habermasian EU looks, on closer inspection, like an Aristotelian republic; hence, perhaps, the Thomist current in his liaison with Pope Benedict XVI. Only the cultivation of virtue may offset the released libidinal-aggressive tendencies of marketised techno-science unfettered in both instrumental modernity and some patterns of globality. Law, rooted in communicative rationality, is the means for achieving such republican virtue. In the Habermasian scheme, is EU modernity the realisation of a secular European Thomism?

Globality, however, offers different historical trajectories to those which concern both enlightened modernists and contra-modernists (conservatives). Whereas modernity may be understood as that which renders the relation between 'system' and 'lifeworld' problematic, 'system' and 'lifeworld' in globality are tangled together across a plurality of socio-technical means. Rather it is the normative, governmental structures that resist these means that are problematic in globality. The globalised lifeworld is not rooted in tradition but in a phenomenology concurrent with socio-technical means. Globality may involve a practical sublation of modernity without at the same time carrying its (enlightened) normative content. This sublation is raised to consciousness in an ergonomic conception of political-economic and social-cultural process – the *uses* made of and by socio-technical networks and whether the *fit* between users and such networks dissipate or enhance vitality. The lifeworld in globality engages a technological condition, whereas in modernity technology is problematised (Ballard, Jünger).

The lifeworld patterns of globality whilst culturally inflected are not specific to cultural traditions. The problem and solution spaces of globality are those of trans-urban existence. Something like a global trans-urban network is emerging which does not simply reinforce geography but rather intersects it and disperses its diverse elements. In short, political-economic systems – whether those of the nation-state or supra-national alliance – begin to be defined relative to non-unitary, dynamic patterns of trans-urban concentration, concatenation and dispersal.

All of this speculation asks whether globality entails the unravelling of the EU by making apparent not only its lack of unity but by revealing its ontology as a network? Whereas law-making and distinguishing boundaries were sufficient for the post World War II era, they are insufficient in the developing era of globality. This would imply that defining the EU in terms of ends – whether external or internal – and using the process of integration (via juridification) to do this may well not only be a forlorn enterprise but one without much conceptual validity. What then is left of the EU? Or for it to do? The *crafting* of means to negotiate globality? In particular, the development of well-formed socio-technical networks for governance that are sufficiently robust to carry populations through the post-national era. In short, the EU stands as a means for negotiating between the dissipation of the nation-states system and the emergence of a globality that appears to be most likely rooted in a global trans-urban network. Only in so far as it comes to redefine itself as a transitional means – between the eras of modernity and globality – can the EU thread itself through and into the complex patterns of governance that are likely to characterise the post-national, globalised world. It can address eurosceptic nation-statism not by federalist, constitutional claims rooted in an ontological unity as a system but by proposing for itself a constitutive role within three trajectories: (i) the emergence of global socio-technical networks, (ii) concurrent with emerging global trans-urban networks, and (iii) the dissipation of the nation-states system. In other words, the EU may seek its sublation in a globality that finishes the project of modernity by raising into consciousness the claims and practical means of a transformed lifeworld. It is this fuller unfolding of the lifeworld, as phenomenology and not tradition, that begins in the era of globality.

Appendix

The writers of social science

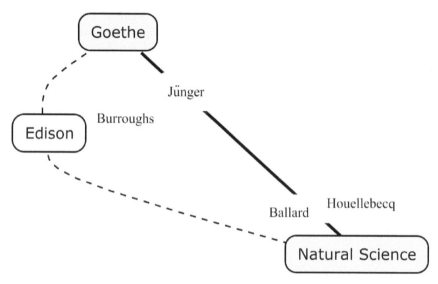

Figure A1.1 The writers of social science

Even more than 'cartographers of disenchantment', the writers discussed in chapter 7 – Ballard, Houellebecq and Jünger – might each be thought of as delineating a 'science of society'. The addition of William S. Burroughs – a friend and predecessor of Ballard's who can also be compared with Jünger and Houellebecq as a theorist of technological society (McLuhan, 1964: 517–19), in his transcendence of the nation-state as a conceptual horizon (McCarthy, 1970: 42), his orientation toward the Maghreb and his renderings of 'the sublime' (among myriad other affinities) – forms a quartet that might profitably be studied in conjunction: 'the writers of social science'. This avenue of research is beyond the scope of the present study; nevertheless, Ballard suggests a way of mapping the terrain. As illustrated by figure A1.1, he assumes a continuum between a 'Goethean' understanding of reality – for which truth is 'in the strict sense a phenomenon – something which appears and can be grasped, specifically, by the sense of sight ... seeing Nature always as something intrinsically inviolable to man's thought' – and, at the opposite pole, a perspective characteristic of natural science as it is understood today, the offspring of luminaries such as Newton and Darwin (Ballard, 1962: 941).

Though a student both of entomology and military science, Jünger identifies strongly with Goethe's perspective (Hervier, 1995: 51). Houellebecq and Ballard, on the other hand, are more comfortable with empiricism, though both are also influenced by modern European thought, from Freud and the surrealists to Huxley and Debord (Hussey, 2002). Finally, Burroughs can be assigned a tangential position, analogous to that of American inventor Thomas Edison (Ballard, 1961, 1962: 941): like Edison, and in contrast to Goethe, Burroughs drew heavily on scientific research and innovation (Kadrey and Stefanac, 1997); however, also like Edison, he lacked a gift for abstract thought, and hence the capacity to systematise the cognitive resources on which he drew – as a consequence, his 'science' was marked by greater disorder and irrationality than those of Ballard and Houellebecq.

References

Adorno, T.W. (1983) *Prisms* (Cambridge, MA: The MIT Press).

Anderson, P. (2006) 'The world made flesh', *New Left Review*, 39, pp. 132–9.

Arendt, H. (1958) *The Human Condition* (Chicago: The University of Chicago Press).

Ashby, W.R. (1956) *An Introduction to Cybernetics* (London: Chapman & Hall).

Ashenden, S. (1998) 'Pluralism within the limits of reason alone? Habermas and the discursive negotiation of consensus', *Critical Review of International Social and Political Philosophy*, 1, pp. 117–36.

Aspinwall, M. and Schneider, G. (2001) 'Institutional research on the European Union: mapping the field', in M. Aspinwall and G. Schneider (eds), *The Rules of Integration: Institutionalist Approaches to the Study of Europe* (Manchester: Manchester University Press).

Ballard, J.G. (1961) 'Practical genius', *Chemistry and Industry*, 20 May 1961.

Ballard, J.G. (1962) 'Last of the Titans', *Chemistry and Industry*, 2 June 1962.

Ballard, J.G. (1967) *The Wind from Nowhere* (London: Penguin).

Ballard, J.G. (1996) *Cocaine Nights* (London: Flamingo).

Ballard, J.G. (2000) *Super-Cannes* (London: Flamingo).

Banchoff, T. and Smith, M.P. (1999) 'Introduction: conceptualising legitimacy in a contested polity', in T. Banchoff and M.P. Smith (eds), *Legitimacy and the European Union: The Contested Polity* (London and New York: Routledge).

Beetham, D. and Lord, C. (1998) *Legitimacy and the European Union* (London and New York: Longman).

Bell, D. (1996) *The Cultural Contradictions of Capitalism* (New York: BasicBooks).

Bellamy, R. and Castiglione, D. (2000a) 'The uses of democracy: reflections on the European democratic deficit', in E.O. Eriksen and E.F. Fossum (eds), *Democracy in the European Union: Integration through Deliberation?* (London and New York: Routledge).

Bellamy, R. and Castiglione, D. (2000b) 'The normative turn in European Union studies: legitimacy, identity, democracy', RUSEL Working Paper No. 38, Department of Politics, University of Exeter, July 2000.

Bellamy, R. and Warleigh, A. (1998) 'From an ethics of integration to an ethics of participation: citizenship and the future of the European Union', *Millennium: Journal of International Studies*, 27, pp. 447–70.

Bey, H. (1994) *Immediatism* (Oakland, CA: AK Press).

Blond, P. (2010) *Red Tory: How Left and Right have Broken Britain and How We can Fix It* (London: Faber & Faber).

Blumenthal, S. (2003) *The Clinton Wars: An Insider's Account of the White House Years* (London: Viking).

Brand, S. (1994) *How Buildings Learn: What Happens after They're Built* (Viking Press: New York).

Burrow, J. (1991) 'Social Darwinism', in D. Miller, J. Coleman, W. Connolly and A. Ryan (eds), *The Blackwell Encyclopaedia of Political Thought* (Oxford: Blackwell).

Caldwell, C. (2004) 'Europe draws back from 1968', *Financial Times*, 26 November 2004.

Caporaso, J.A. (2000) *The European Union: Dilemmas of Regional Integration* (London: Westview).

Carleheden, M. and Gabriëls, R. (1996) 'An interview with Jürgen Habermas', *Theory, Culture and Society*, 13(3), pp. 1–17.

Castells, M. (1999) 'The unification of Europe: globalisation, identity, and the network state', in *End of Millenium*, Volume III of *The Information Age: Economy, Society, Culture* (UK: Blackwell).

Checkel, J.T. (2001) 'Social construction and European integration', in T. Christiansen, K.E. Jørgensen and A. Wiener (eds), *The Social Construction of Europe* (London: Sage).

Christiansen, T., Jørgensen, K.E. and Wiener, A. (2001) 'Introduction', in T. Christiansen, K.E. Jørgensen and A. Wiener (eds), *The Social Construction of Europe* (London: Sage).

Chryssochoou, D. (2000) 'Meta-theory and the study of the European Union: capturing the normative turn', *Journal of European Integration*, 22(2), pp. 123–44.

Cilliers, P. (2000) *Complexity and Postmodernism: Understanding Complex Systems* (London: Routledge).

Cohen, R.S. and Wartofsky, M.W. (1980) 'Editorial preface', in H.R. Maturana and F.J. Varela, *Autopoiesis and Cognition: The Realisation of the Living* (Netherlands: D. Reidel).

Comite des Sages (1996) *For a Europe of Civic and Social Rights* (Office for Official Publications of the European Communities).

Commission of the European Communities (2001) *European Governance*, White Paper, available at: http://eur-lex.europa.eu/LexUriServ/site/en/com/2001/com2001 _0428en01.pdf (accessed 31 March 2011).

Coudenhove-Kalergi, R. (1923) *Pan-Europa* (Wien: Pan-Europa-Verlag).

Cram, L. (1997) *Policy-Making in the EU: Conceptual Lenses and the Integration Process* (London and New York: Routledge).

Cram, L. (1998) 'Integration theory and the study of the European policy process', in J. Richardson (ed.), *European Union: Power and Policymaking* (London and New York: Routledge).

Davis, D. (2009) 'I wouldn't trust Google with my personal info', *The Times*, 27 July 2009, available at: http://www.timesonline.co.uk/tol/comment/columnists/guest _contributors/article6728116.ece (accessed 27 July 2009).

Davis, M. (2004) 'Planet of slums', *New Left Review*, 26, pp. 5–34.

Dawkins, R. (2006) *The God Delusion* (London: Bantham).

d'Entrèves, M.P. (1996) 'Introduction', in M.P. d'Entrèves and S. Benhabib (eds), *Habermas and the Unfinished Project of Modernity* (Cambridge: Polity).

Diez, T. (2001) 'Speaking "Europe": the politics of integration discourse', in T. Christiansen, K.E. Jørgensen and A. Wiener (eds), *The Social Construction of Europe* (London: Sage).

Durkheim, É. (1951) *Suicide: A Study in Sociology* (Glencoe, IL: Free Press).

Duvenage, P. (2003) *Habermas and Aesthetics: The Limits of Communicative Reason* (Cambridge: Polity).

Dyzenhaus, D. (2002) 'Hermann Heller: Introduction', in A.J. Jacobson and B. Schlink (eds), *Weimar: A Jurisprudence of Crisis* (Berkeley, CA: University of California Press).

Edwards, J. (2003) 'Evolutionary psychology and politics', *Economy and Society*, 32(2), pp. 280–98.

Engelbrekt, K. (2002) 'Multiple asymmetries: the European Union's neo-Byzantine approach to Eastern enlargement', *Journal of International Politics*, 39(1), pp. 37–51, available at: www.statsvet.su.se/stv_hemsida/statsvetenskap_kjell_engelbrekt_right. htm (accessed 24 July 2005).

Eriksen, E.O. (2005) 'Reflexive integration in Europe', in E.O. Eriksen (ed.), *Making the European Polity: Reflexive Integration in the EU* (London and New York: Routledge).

Eriksen, E.O. (2009) *The Unfinished Democratisation of Europe* (Oxford: Oxford University Press).

Eriksen, E.O. and Fossum, E.F. (2000) 'Post-national integration', in E.O. Eriksen and E.F. Fossum (eds), *Democracy in the European Union: Integration through Deliberation?* (London and New York: Routledge).

Eurobarometer (2002) 57, Spring 2002, available at: http://ec.europa.eu/public _opinion/archives/eb/eb57/eb57_en.pdf (accessed 25 May 2005).

European Commission (2001) *European Governance: A White Paper*, COM(2001) 428 (Luxembourg: Office of Official Publications of the European Communities).

European Parliament and Council of Ministers (1995) 'Directive of the European Parliament and of the Council of 24 October 1995 on the protection of individuals with regard to the processing of personal data and on the free movement of such data', *Official Journal of the European Communities*, No. L 281/31, 23 November 1995, available at: http://ec.europa.eu/justice/policies/privacy/docs/95-46-ce/dir1995-46 _part1_en.pdf (accessed 25 May 2005).

Fidler, S. and Baker, G. (2003) 'America's democratic imperialists', *Financial Times*, 5 March 2003.

Fink, J., Lewis, G. and Clarke, J. (eds) (2001) *Rethinking European Welfare: Transformations of Europe and Social Policy* (London: Sage).

Foucault, M. (1990) 'Critical theory/intellectual history', in L. Kritzman (ed.), *Politics, Philosophy, Culture: Interviews and Other Writings of Michel Foucault, 1977–1984* (London and New York: Routledge).

Fukuyama, F. (1989) 'The end of history?', *The National Interest*, Summer, pp. 3–18.

Geyer, R. (2000) *Exploring European Social Policy* (Cambridge: Polity).

Geyer, R. (2003) 'European integration, the problem of complexity and the revision of theory', *Journal of Common Market Studies*, 41, pp. 15–35.

Gibson, W. (1984) *Neuromancer* (New York: Ace Books).

Giddens, A. (1998) *The Third Way: The Renewal of Social Democracy* (Cambridge: Polity).

Giddens, A. and Hutton, W. (2000) 'Fighting back', in A. Giddens and W. Hutton (eds), *On the Edge: Living with Global Capitalism* (London: Jonathan Cape).

Glazov, J. (2003) 'Frontpage interview: Christopher Hitchens', *FrontPageMag.Com*, 10 December 2003, available at: http://97.74.65.51/readArticle.aspx?ARTID=15054 (accessed 22 May 2010).

Goff, J. (1992) *The Last Days of the Most Hidden Man* (Kindle Edition: Amazon Media).

Goff, J. (2008) 'What price privacy?', *Philosophy Now*, 66 (March/April), pp. 6–7.

Golding, W. (1961) *The Inheritors* (London: Faber & Faber).

Golding, W. (1986) *Lord of the Flies* (London: Faber & Faber).

Goodhart, D. (2004) 'Too diverse?', *Prospect*, February 2004.

Goodrick-Clarke, N. (2002) *Black Sun: Aryan Cults, Esoteric Nazism, and the Politics of Identity* (New York University Press).

Gorz, A. (1980) *Adieux au proletariat: Au-delà du socialisme* (Paris: Éditions Galilée). Tr. as (1982) *Farewell to the Working Class: An Essay on Post-Industrial Socialism* (London: Pluto Press).

Gorz, A. (1981) 'Nine theses for a future left', *Telos*, 48, pp. 91–8.

Gray, J. (1998) *False Dawn: The Delusions of Global Capitalism* (London: Granta Books).

Gray, J. (2002) *Straw Dogs: Thoughts on Humans and Other Animals* (London: Granta Books).

Gray, J. (2003) *Al Qaeda and What It Means to be Modern* (London: Faber & Faber).

Gray, J. (2004a) *Heresies: Against Progress and Other Illusions* (London: Granta Books).

Gray, J. (2004b) 'Ethically engineered', *Times Literary Supplement*, 16 January 2004.

Gray, J. (2007) *Black Mass: Apocalyptic Religion and the Death of Utopia* (London: Allen Lane).

Gray, J. (2010) 'Progressive, like the 1980s', *London Review of Books*, 21 October 2010.

Grewal, S.S. (2001) 'The paradox of integration: Habermas and the unfinished project of European Union', *Politics*, 21(2), pp. 114–23.

Grewal, S.S. (2005) 'A cosmopolitan Europe by constitutional means? Assessing the theoretical foundations of Habermas' political prescriptions', *Journal of European Integration*, 27(2), pp. 191–215.

Grewal, S.S. (2010) 'Habermas, law and European social policy: a rejoinder to Murphy', *Journal of European Public Policy*, 17(2), pp. 282–98.

Griffin, R.D. (1993) *The Nature of Fascism* (London: Routledge).

Haas, E.B. (1958) *The Uniting of Europe: Political, Social, and Economic Forces 1950–1957* (California: Stanford University Press).

Haas, E.B. (1964) *Beyond the Nation-State: Functionalism and International Organisation* (California: Stanford University Press).

Haas, E.B. (1975) *The Obsolescence of Regional Integration Theory*, Berkeley: University of California, Institute of International Studies, Research Series No. 25.

Haas, E.B. (2001) 'Does constructivism subsume neo-functionalism?', in T. Christiansen, K.E. Jørgensen and A. Wiener (eds), *The Social Construction of Europe* (London: Sage).

Habermas, J. (1962) *Strukturwandel der Öffentlichkeit – Untersuchungen zu einer Kategorie der bürgerlichen Gesellschaft* (Neuwied/Berlin: Hermann Luchterhand Verlag). Tr. as (1989) *The Structural Transformation of the Public Sphere: An Inquiry into a Category of Bourgeois Society* (Cambridge, MA: The MIT Press).

Habermas, J. (1973) 'What does a crisis mean today? Legitimation problems in late capitalism', *Social Research*, 40, pp. 643–67.

Habermas, J. (1973) *Legitimationsprobleme im Spätkapitalismus* (Frankfurt: Suhrkamp). Tr. as (1975) *Legitimation Crisis* (Boston: Beacon Press).

Habermas, J. (1981) *Theorie des kommunikativen Handelns*, Zwei Bände (Frankfurt: Suhrkamp). Tr. as *The Theory of Communicative Action*, (1984) volume 1 and (1987) volume 2 (Cambridge: Polity).

Habermas, J. (1981a) 'New social movements', *Telos*, 49, pp. 33–7.

Habermas, J. (1981b) 'Modernity versus postmodernity', *New German Critique*, 22, pp. 3–14.

Habermas, J. (1985) *Die neue Unübersichtlichkeit* (Frankfurt: Suhrkamp). Tr. as (1989) *The New Conservatism* (Cambridge: Polity).

Habermas, J. (1985) *Der Philosophische Diskurs der Moderne* (Frankfurt: Suhrkamp). Tr. as (1990) *The Philosophical Discourse of Modernity* (Cambridge: Polity).

Habermas, J. (1986a) 'Political experience and the renewal of Marxist theory', in Peter Dews (ed.), *Autonomy and Solidarity* (London: Verso).

Habermas, J. (1986b) 'Conservatism and capitalist crisis', in Peter Dews (ed.), *Autonomy and Solidarity* (London: Verso).

Habermas, J. (1986c) 'The dialectics of rationalisation', in Peter Dews (ed.), *Autonomy and Solidarity* (London: Verso).

Habermas, J. (1986d) 'Conservative politics, work, socialism and Utopia today', in Peter Dews (ed.), *Autonomy and Solidarity* (London: Verso).

Habermas, J. (1990a) 'What does socialism mean today? The rectifying revolution and the need for new thinking on the left', *New Left Review*, 183, pp. 3–21.

Habermas, J. (1990b) *On the Logic of the Social Sciences* (Cambridge: Polity).

Habermas, J. (1992) *Faktizität und Geltung* (Frankfurt: Suhrkamp). Tr. as (1996) *Between Facts and Norms* (Cambridge: Polity).

Habermas, J. (1992a) 'Citizenship and national identity: some reflections on the future of Europe', *Praxis International*, 12(1), pp. 1–19.

Habermas, J. (1994a) 'The normative deficits of unification', in *The Past as Future: Jürgen Habermas Interviewed by Michael Haller* (Cambridge: Polity).

Habermas, J. (1994b) 'Neoconservative cultural criticism in the United States and West

Germany', in Shierry Weber Nicholsen (ed.), *The New Conservatism: Cultural Criticism and the Historians' Debate* (Cambridge: Polity).

Habermas, J. (1994c) 'The new obscurity: the crisis of the welfare state and the exhaustion of utopian energies', in Shierry Weber Nicholsen (ed.), *The New Conservatism: Cultural Criticism and the Historians' Debate* (Cambridge: Polity).

Habermas, J. (1994d) 'Historical consciousness and post-traditional identity: the federal republic's orientation to the West', in Shierry Weber Nicholsen (ed.), *The New Conservatism: Cultural Criticism and the Historians' Debate* (Cambridge: Polity).

Habermas, J. (1994e) 'Modern and postmodern architecture', in Shierry Weber Nicholsen (ed.), *The New Conservatism: Cultural Criticism and the Historians' Debate* (Cambridge: Polity).

Habermas, J. (1994f) 'The horrors of autonomy: Carl Schmitt in English', in Shierry Weber Nicholsen (ed.), *The New Conservatism: Cultural Criticism and the Historians' Debate* (Cambridge: Polity).

Habermas, J. (1995) *The Theory of Communicative Action, Volume II: The Critique of Functionalist Reason* (Cambridge: Polity).

Habermas, J. (1996a) 'Modernity: an unfinished project', in M.P. d'Entrèves and S. Benhabib (eds), *Habermas and the Unfinished Project of Modernity* (Cambridge: Polity).

Habermas, J. (1996b) *Postmetaphysical Thinking: Philosophical Essays* (Cambridge, MA: The MIT Press).

Habermas, J. (1997a) *The Theory of Communicative Action, Volume I: Reason and the Rationalisation of Society* (Cambridge: Polity).

Habermas, J. (1997b) 'Reply to Grimm', in P. Gowan and P. Anderson (eds), *The Question of Europe* (London: Verso).

Habermas, J. (1998) *Die postnationale Konstellation – Politische Essays* (Frankfurt: Suhrkamp). Tr. as (2001) *The Postnational Constellation: Political Essays* (Cambridge: Polity).

Habermas, J. (1998a) *The Philosophical Discourse of Modernity: Twelve Lectures* (Cambridge: Polity).

Habermas, J. (1998b) *Between Facts and Norms: Contributions toward a Discourse Theory of Law and Democracy* (Cambridge: Polity).

Habermas, J. (1998c) 'There are alternatives', *New Left Review*, 231, pp. 3–12.

Habermas, J. (1998d) *A Berlin Republic: Writings on Germany* (Cambridge: Polity).

Habermas, J. (1998e) 'Learning by disaster? A diagnostic look back on the short 20th century', *Constellations*, 5(3), pp. 307–20.

Habermas, J. (1998f) 'The European nation-state: on the past and future of sovereignty and citizenship', *Public Culture*, 10(2), pp. 397–416.

Habermas, J. (1999a) 'The European nation-state and the pressures of globalisation', *New Left Review*, 235, pp. 46–59.

Habermas, J. (1999b) *The Inclusion of the Other: Studies in Political Theory* (Cambridge, MA: The MIT Press).

Habermas, J. (2000) 'Beyond the nation-state?: on some consequences of economic globalisation', in E.O. Eriksen and E.F. Fossum (eds), *Democracy in the European Union: Integration through Deliberation?* (London and New York: Routledge).

Habermas, J. (2001a) 'A constitution for Europe?', *New Left Review*, 11, pp. 5–26.

Habermas, J. (2001b) *On the Pragmatics of Social Interaction: Preliminary Studies in the Theory of Communicative Action* (Cambridge, MA: The MIT Press).

Habermas, J. (2001c) *The Postnational Constellation: Political Essays* (Cambridge: Polity Press).

Habermas, J. (2002) 'Letter to America', *The Nation*, December 2002, available at: http://www.thenation.com/doc.mhtml?i=20021216&s=habermas (accessed 24 May 2003).

Habermas, J. (2003a) 'Interpreting the fall of a monument', *Constellations*, 10(3), pp. 364–70.

Habermas, J. (2003b) 'A dialogue with Jürgen Habermas', in G. Borradori (ed.), *Philosophy in a Time of Terror: Dialogues with Jürgen Habermas and Jacques Derrida* (Chicago and London: University of Chicago).

Habermas, J. (2004) 'America and the world: a conversation with Jürgen Habermas', *Logos*, 3(3).

Habermas, J. (2005) 'The illusory "Leftist No": adopting the constitution to strengthen Europe's power to act', in *signandsight*, May 2005, available at: http://www.signandsight.com/features/163.html (accessed 25 May 2005). This article was originally published in French in the *Nouvel Observateur*, 7 May 2005.

Habermas, J. (2008a) 'And the wheels stopped turning', *Spiegel Online International*, available at: http://www.spiegel.de/international/europe/0,1518,560549,00.html (accessed 13 October 2008).

Habermas, J. (2008b) 'Der Hermann Heller der frühen Bundesrepublik Wolfgang Abendroth zum 100. Geburtstag', in *Ach, Europa. Kleine politische Schriften XI* (Frankfurt: Suhrkamp Verlag).

Habermas, J. (2008c) 'Religion in the public sphere', available at: http://www.sandiego.edu/pdf/pdf_library/habermaslecture031105_c939cceb2ab087bdfc6df291ec0fc3fa.PDF (accessed 8 May 2010).

Habermas, J. (2009) *Europe: The Faltering Project* (Cambridge: Polity).

Habermas, J. and Derrida, J. (2003) 'February 15th, or what binds Europeans together: a plea for a common foreign policy, beginning in the core of Europe', *Constellations*, 10(3), pp. 291–7.

Habermas, J. and Ratzinger, J. (2006) *The Dialectics of Secularisation: On Reason and Religion* (San Francisco, CA: Ignatius).

Hardt, M. and Negri, A. (2000) *Empire* (Cambridge, MA: Harvard University Press).

Hatoyama, Y. (2009) 'My political philosophy', *Financial Times*, 13 August 2009.

Hawken, P., Lovins, A. and Lovins, L. (1999) *Natural Capitalism: The Next Industrial Revolution* (London: Earthscan Publications).

Heidegger, M. (1977) *The Question Concerning Technology and Other Essays* (New York: Harper & Row).

Heinsohn, G. (2008) *Söhne und Weltmacht: Terror im Aufstieg und Fall der Nationen* (Munich: Piper).

Heller, H. (2002) 'Political democracy and social homogeneity', in A.J. Jacobson and B. Schlink (eds), *Weimar: A Jurisprudence of Crisis* (Berkeley, CA: University of California Press).

Hervier, J. (1995) *The Details of Time: Conversations with Jünger* (New York: Marsilio Publishers).

Hesse, H. (1943) *Das Glasperlenspiel* (Zürich: Fretz & Wasmuth). Tr. as (1973) *The Glass Bead Game* (London: Penguin).

Heylighen, F. and Joslyn, C. (2001) 'Cybernetics and second-order cybernetics', in R.A. Meyers (ed.), *Encyclopedia of Physical Science and Technology* (New York: Academic Press).

Hitchens, C. (2007) *God Is Not Great: How Religion Poisons Everything* (New York: Twelve Books).

Hix, S. (1994) 'The study of the European Community: the challenge to comparative politics', *West European Politics*, 17(1), pp. 1–30.

Hix, S. (1998) 'The study of the European Union II: the "new governance" agenda and its rival', *Journal of European Public Policy*, 5, pp. 38–65.

Hix, S. (1999) *The Political System of the European Union* (London: Palgrave).

Hobbes, T. (2000) *Leviathan* (Cambridge: Cambridge University Press).

Hoffman, S. (1995) 'Obstinate or obsolete? France, European integration and the fate of the nation state', in S. Hoffman, *The European Sisyphus: Essays on Europe 1964–1994* (Oxford: Westview Press).

Hollis, M. and Smith, S. (1991) *Explaining and Understanding International Relations* (Oxford: Clarendon Press).

Holub, R.C. (2006) *Jürgen Habermas: Critic in the Public Sphere* (London and New York: Routledge).

Honneth, A. (2005) 'Reification: a recognition-theoretical view', *The Tanner Lectures on Human Values*, March 2005, available at: http://www.tannerlectures.utah.edu /lectures/documents/Honneth_2006.pdf (accessed 2 February 2011).

Hooghe, L. and Marks, G. (2001) *Multi-Level Governance and European Integration* (Lanham: Rowman & Littlefield).

Horkheimer, M. and Adorno, T.W. (2002) *Dialectic of Enlightenment: Philosophical Fragments* (California: Stanford University Press).

Houellebecq, M. (1998) *Les particules élémentaires* (Paris: Flammarion). Tr. as (2001) *Atomised* (London: Vintage).

Houellebecq, M. (2001) *Platforme* (Paris: Flammarion). Tr. as (2003) *Platform* (London: Vintage).

Houellebecq, M. (2001a) *Atomised* (London: Vintage).

Huntington, S. (1996) *The Clash of Civilisations and the Remaking of the World Order* (New York: Simon & Schuster).

Hussey, A. (2002) 'The pornographer's manifesto', *New Statesman*, 19 August 2002, available at: http://www.newstatesman.com/200208190026 (accessed 23 May 2010).

Joerges, C. (2003) 'Europe as Großraum? Shifting legal conceptualisations of the integration project', in C. Joerges and N.S. Ghaleigh (eds), *Darker Legacies of Law in Europe: The Shadow of National Socialism and Fascism over Europe and its Legal Traditions* (Oxford: Hart).

Joerges, C. (2004) 'What is left of the European Economic Constitution?', EUI Working Paper (Law), 04/13, available at: http://cadmus.eui.eu/dspace/bitstream/1814/2828/1 /law04–13.pdf (accessed 15 March 2010).

Joerges, C. and Castiglione, D. (2005) 'Working through "Bitter Experiences" towards constitutionalisation: a critique of the disregard for history in European constitutional theory: are those that forget the past doomed to repeat its mistakes? A comment on Christian Joerges', *EUI Working Paper*, Law No. 2005/14, Department of Law, European University Institute, available at: http://cadmus.iue.it/dspace/bitstream/

Johnson, J. (2004) 'Caste out', *Financial Times*, 17 December 2004.

Josipovici, G. (2010) 'Modernism still matters', *New Statesman*, 6 September 2010, available at: http://www.newstatesman.com/books/2010/09/writers-english-modernism (accessed 6 November 2010).

Jospin, L. (2002) 'My vision of Europe and globalisation', in F. Michel (ed.), *My Vision of Europe and Globalisation: Lionel Jospin* (Cambridge: Polity).

Judt, T. (2005) *Postwar: A History of Europe since 1945* (New York: Penguin).

Jünger, E. (1939) *Auf den Marmorklippen* (Hamburg: Hanseatische Verlagsanstalt). Tr. as (1970) *On the Marble Cliffs* (London: Penguin).

Jünger, E. (1977) *Eumeswil* (Stuttgart: Klett-Cotta).

Jünger, E. (1993) *Aladdin's Problem* (London: Quartet Books).

Kadrey, R. and Stefanac, S. (1997) 'J.G. Ballard on William S. Burroughs' naked truth', *Salon*, September 1997, available at: http://www.salon.com/sept97/wsb970902.html.

Kagan, R. (2003) *Of Paradise and Power: America and Europe in the New World Order* (New York: Knopf).

Kaiser, W. (2007) *Christian Democracy and the Origins of the European Union* (Cambridge: Cambridge University Press).

Keegan, W. (1993) *The Spectre of Capitalism: The Future of the World Economy after the Fall of Communism* (New York: Vintage).

Kirino, N. (2004) *Out* (London: Vintage).

Kirino, N. (2008) *Grotesque* (London: Vintage).

Lange, P. (1992) 'The politics of the social dimension', in A. Sbragia (ed.), *Euro-Politics* (Washington, DC: Brookings Institution).

Latour, B. (1993) *We Have Never Been Modern* (New York: Harvester & Wheatsheaf).

Leibfried, S. (2005) 'Social policy: left to the judges and the markets?', in H. Wallace and W. Wallace (eds), *Policy-Making in the European Union* (Oxford: Oxford University Press).

Leibfried, S. (2010) 'Social policy: left to the judges and the markets?', in H. Wallace, M.A. Pollack and A.R. Young (eds), *Policy-Making in the European Union* (Oxford: Oxford University Press).

Leibfried, S. and Pierson, P. (1995a) 'Multitiered institutions and the making of social policy', in S. Leibfried and P. Pierson (eds), *European Social Policy: Between Fragmentation and Integration* (Washington, DC: Brookings Institution).

Leibfried, S. and Pierson, P. (1995b) 'Semisovereign welfare states: social policy in a multi-tiered Europe', in S. Leibfried and P. Pierson (eds), *European Social Policy: Between Fragmentation and Integration* (Washington, DC: Brookings Institution).

Leibfried, S. and Pierson, P. (1995c) 'The dynamics of social policy integration', in S. Leibfried and P. Pierson (eds), *European Social Policy: Between Fragmentation and Integration* (Washington, DC: Brookings Institution).

Leibfried, S. and Pierson, P. (2000) 'Social policy', in H. Wallace and W. Wallace (eds), *Policy-Making in the European Union* (Oxford: Oxford University Press).

Leonard, M. (2005) 'Europe and VISA: separated at birth?', *The Globalist*, 1 April 2005, available at: http://www.theglobalist.com/StoryId.aspx?StoryId=4463 (accessed 13 May 2010).

Lévy, B. (2007) 'Europe is possible', in *signandsight*, April 2007, available at: http://www.signandsight.com/features/1305.html (accessed 23 May 2010).

Lewin, M. (1975) *Political Undercurrents in Soviet Economic Debates* (London: Pluto Press).

Lovelock, J. (2007) *The Revenge of Gaia* (London: Penguin).

Luke, T. (2006) 'Alterity or antimodernism: a response to Versluis', *Telos*, 137, pp. 131–42.

Luhmann, N. (1995) *Social Systems* (Stanford, CA: Stanford University Press).

Machiavelli, N. (1970) *The Prince* (London: Penguin).

MacIntyre, A. (1963) 'Going into Europe', *Encounter*, 20, p. 65.

Majone, G. (1992) 'The European Community between social policy and social regulation', EUI Working Papers, 92/27.

Majone, G. (1995) 'The development of social regulation in the European Community', EUI Working Papers, 95/2.

Majone, G. (1996) *Regulating Europe* (London and New York: Routledge).

Marcus, G. (1989) *Lipstick Traces: A Secret History of the Twentieth Century* (London: Secker & Warburg).

Maturana, H.R. (1978) 'Cognition', in P.M. Hejl, K.K. Wolfram and R. Gerhard (eds), *Wahrnehmung und Kommunikation* (Frankfurt: Peter Lang).

Maturana, H.R. and Varela, F.J. (1980) *Autopoiesis and Cognition: The Realisation of the Living* (Netherlands: D. Reidel).

Matuštík, M.B. (2001) *Jürgen Habermas: A Philosophical-Political Profile* (Lanham: Rowman & Littlefield).

Mazey, S. (1996) 'The development of the European idea: from sectoral integration to political union', in J. Richardson (ed.), *European Union: Power and Policymaking* (London and New York: Routledge).

McCarthy, M. (1970) *The Writing on the Wall and Other Literary Essays* (London: Lowe and Brydone).

McCarthy, T. (1978) *The Critical Theory of Jürgen Habermas* (London: Hutchinson).

McCarthy, T. (1997) 'Translator's introduction', in J. Habermas, *The Theory of Communicative Action, Volume I: Reason and the Rationalisation of Society* (Cambridge: Polity).

McCormick, J.P. (2007) *Weber, Habermas, and Transformations of the European State: Constitutional, Social, and Supranational Democracy* (Cambridge: Cambridge University Press).

McLuhan, M. (1964) 'Notes on Burroughs', *The Nation*, 28 December 1964, pp. 517–19.

Medina, E. (2006) 'Designing freedom, regulating a nation: socialist cybernetics in Allende's Chile', *Journal of Latin American Studies*, 38, pp. 571–606.

Menand, L. (2002) 'What comes naturally: does evolution explain who we are?', *The New Yorker*, 25 November 2002, available at: http://www.newyorker.com/archive /2002/11/25/021125crbo_books (accessed 18 February 2010).

Mendieta, E. (2002) 'Introduction', in J. Habermas, *Religion and Rationality: Essays on Reason, God, and Modernity* (Cambridge: Polity).

Micklethwait, J. and Wooldridge, A. (2004) *The Right Nation: Why America is Different* (London: Allen Lane).

Milward, A.S. (2000) *The European Rescue of the Nation-State* (London and New York: Routledge).

Mingers, J. (1995) *Self-Producing Systems: Implications and Applications of Autopoiesis* (New York and London: Plenum Press).

Mitterrand, F. (1995) 'Geburtstagsrede für Ernst Jünger: Hier ist ein Freier Mensch', *Frankfurter Allgemeine Zeitung*, 29 March 1995.

Moravcsik, A (1991) 'Negotiating the Single European Act', in R.O. Keohane and S. Hoffman (eds), *The New European Community: Decision Making and Institutional Change* (Boulder, CO: Westview).

Moravcsik, A. (1993) 'Preferences and power in the European Community: a liberal inter-governmental approach', *Journal of Common Market Studies*, 31, pp. 473–524.

Moravcsik, A. (2001) 'Constructivism and European integration: a critique', in T. Christiansen, K.E. Jørgensen and A. Wiener (eds), *The Social Construction of Europe* (London: Sage).

Moravcsik, A. (2002) 'In defence of the 'democratic deficit': reassessing legitimacy in the European Union', *Journal of Common Market Studies*, 40(4), pp. 603–24.

Moravcsik, A. (2005) 'A category error', *Prospect*, July 2005.

Müller, J.W. (2001) 'Portrait: Jürgen Habermas', *Prospect*, March 2001.

Münchau, W. (2004) 'Bush II could be good for Europe', *Financial Times*, 7 November 2004.

Münchau, W. (2010) 'Why Greece will default', *Financial Times*, 7 April 2010.

Murphy, M. (2005) 'Between facts, norms and a post-national constellation: Habermas, law and European social policy', *Journal of European Public Policy*, 12, pp. 143–56.

Murray, N. (1989) 'Anti-racists and other demons: the press and ideology in Thatcher's Britain', in *Racism and the Press in Thatcher's Britain* (London: Institute of Race Relations).

Neunreither, K. (1994) 'The democratic deficit of the European Union: towards closer cooperation between the European Parliament and the National Parliaments', *Government and Opposition*, 29, pp. 299–314.

Nietzsche, F. (1990) *Beyond Good and Evil: Prelude to a Philosophy of the Future* (London: Penguin).

Obradovic, D. (1996) 'Policy legitimacy and the EU', *Journal of Common Market Studies*, 34, pp. 191–221.

Offe, C. (2000) 'The democratic welfare state in an integrating Europe', in M.T. Greven and L.W. Pauly (eds), *Democracy Beyond the State? The European Dilemma and the Emerging Global Order* (Lanham: Rowman & Littlefield).

Outhwaite, W. (1996) 'General introduction', in W. Outhwaite (ed.), *The Habermas Reader* (Cambridge: Polity).

Padoa-Schioppa, T. (2010) 'Euro remains on the right side of history', *Financial Times*, 13 May 2010.

Parry, R. (1995) 'Redefining the welfare state', in J. Hayward and E.C. Page (eds), *Governing the New Europe* (Cambridge: Polity).

Parsons, T. (1937) *The Structure of Social Action* (New York: McGraw-Hill).

Parsons, T. (1999) 'Christianity and modern industrial society', in B.S. Turner (ed.), *The Talcott Parsons Reader* (UK: Blackwell).

Peel, Q. (2004a) 'Europe steals Washington's diplomatic clothes', *Financial Times*, 10 February 2004.

Peel, Q. (2004b) 'Euroscepticism spreads to the west', *Financial Times*, 2 December 2004.

Petit, C. (1993) *Robinson* (London: Jonathan Cape).

Pinker, S. (2002) *The Blank Slate: The Modern Denial of Human Nature* (London: Allen Lane).

Polanyi, K. (1944) *The Great Transformation: The Political and Economic Origins of Our Time* (New York: Farrar & Rinehart).

Puchala, D. (1972) 'Of blind men, elephants, and international integration', *Journal of Common Market Studies*, (10)3, pp. 267–84.

Reck-Malleczewen, F. (2000) *Diary of a Man in Despair* (London: Duck Editions).

Rees, M. (2003) *Our Final Century: Will the Human Race Survive the Twenty-First Century?* (Harlow, UK: Heinemann)

Rosamond, B. (2000) *Theories of European Integration* (Basingstoke, UK: Palgrave).

Ross, G. (1995) *Jacques Delors and European Integration* (Cambridge: Polity).

Sandholtz, W. and Zysman, J. (1989) '1992: recasting the European bargain', *World Politics*, 42, pp. 95–128.

Sassen, S. (2001) *The Global City: New York, London, Tokyo* (Princeton, NJ: Princeton University Press).

Scharpf, F. (1998) 'Negative and positive integration in the political economy of European welfare states', in G. Marks, F.W. Scharpf, P. Schmitter and W. Steeck (eds), *Governance in the European Union* (London: Sage).

Scharpf, F. (1999) *Governing in Europe: Effective and Democratic?* (Oxford: Oxford University Press).

Schlesinger, P. and Kevin, D. (2000) 'Can the European Union become a sphere of publics?', in E.O. Eriksen and E.F. Fossum (eds), *Democracy in the European Union: Integration through Deliberation?* (London and New York: Routledge).

Schmitter, P.C. (1998a) 'Examining the present Euro-polity with the help of past theories', in G. Marks, F.W. Scharpf, P. Schmitter and W. Steeck (eds), *Governance in the European Union* (London: Sage).

Schmitter, P.C. (1998b) 'Imagining the future of the Euro-polity with the help of new concepts', in G. Marks, F.W. Scharpf, P. Schmitter and W. Steeck (eds), *Governance in the European Union* (London: Sage).

Schmitter, P.C. (2000) *How to Democratize the European Union ... And Why Bother?* (Lanham: Roman & Littlefield).

Schmitter, P.C. (2002) 'Neo-neo-functionalism: déjà vu, all over again?', European University Institute, unpublished paper, available at: http://www.iue.it/SPS /People/Faculty/CurrentProfessors/PDFFiles/SchmitterPDFfiles/Neoneofunctionalism. pdf (accessed 13 August 2004).

Schuller, F. (2006) 'Foreword', in J. Habermas and J. Ratzinger, *The Dialectics of Secularisation: On Reason and Religion* (San Francisco, CA: Ignatius).

Shaw, J. (2001) 'Postnational constitutionalism in the European Union', in T.

Christiansen, K.E. Jørgensen and A. Wiener (eds), *The Social Construction of Europe* (London: Sage).

Shiller, R. (2003) *The New Financial Order: Risk in the 21st Century* (Princeton, NJ: Princeton University Press).

Shortt, R. (2010) 'So far and yet so near', *The Tablet*, 11 September 2010.

Siedentop, L. (2000) *Democracy in Europe* (London: Penguin).

Siedentop, L. (2005) 'A crisis of legitimacy', *Prospect*, July 2005.

Singer, D. (1961) 'The level-of-analysis problem in international relations', in K. Knorr and S. Verba (eds), *The International System* (Princeton, NJ: Princeton University Press).

Sinkin, R. (2004) 'The EU and US: from cooperation to rivalry', *Journal of European Integration*, 26(1), pp. 93–100.

Smith, M.P. (1999) 'EU Legitimacy and the "defensive" reaction to the single European market', in T. Banchoff and M.P. Smith (eds), *Legitimacy and the European Union: The Contested Polity* (London and New York: Routledge).

Sokal, A. and Bricmont, J. (1997) *Impostures intellectuelles* (Paris: Éditions Odile Jacob). Tr. as (1998) *Intellectual Impostures* (London: Profile Books).

Sontag, S. (1964) 'Notes on "Camp"', *Partisan Review*, 31(4), pp. 515–530.

Spengler, O. (1918) *Der Untergang des Abendlandes, Gestalt und Wirklichkeit* (Munich: C.H. Beck Verlag). Tr. as (1926) *The Decline of the West, Volume 1: Form and Actuality* (New York: Knopf).

Spengler (2009) 'Overcoming ethnicity', *Asia Times Online*, 6 January 2009, available at: http://www.atimes.com/atimes/Front_Page/KA06Aa01.html (accessed 9 May 2010).

Steiner, G. (1970) 'Introduction', in E. Jünger, *On the Marble Cliffs* (London: Penguin).

Streeck, W. (1998) 'Neo-voluntarism: a new European social policy regime?', in G. Marks, F.W. Scharpf, P. Schmitter and W. Steeck (eds), *Governance in the European Union* (London: Sage).

Streeck, W. and Schmitter, P.C. (1991) 'From national corporatism to transnational pluralism: organised interests in the Single European Market', *Politics and Society*, 19(2), pp. 133–65.

Therborn, G. (1997) 'Europe in the twenty-first century: the world's Scandinavia', in P. Gowan and P. Anderson (eds), *The Question of Europe* (London: Verso).

Therborn, G. (2009) 'NATO's demographer', *New Left Review*, 56, available at: http://www.newleftreview.org/?view=2775 (accessed 23 May 2010).

Time (1943) 'One Europe', 29 November 1943, available at: http://www.time.com/time/magazine/article/0,9171,791166-1,00.html (accessed 25 May 2005).

Trenz, H. and de Wilde, P. (2009) 'Denouncing European integration: Euroscepticism as a reactive identity formation', *RECON Online Working Paper Series*, 2009/10, available at: http://www.reconproject.eu/main.php/RECON_wp_0910.pdf?fileitem=16662597 (accessed 23 May 2010).

van Kranenburg, R. (1999) 'Whose Gramsci? Right-wing Gramscism', *International Gramsci Society Newsletter*, 9, pp. 14–18, available at: http://www.internationalgramscisociety.org/igsn/index.html (accessed 3 May 2010).

Versluis, A. (2006) 'Antimodernism', *Telos*, 137, pp. 96–130.

Virilio, P. (1977) *Vitesse et Politique* (Paris: Éditions Galilée). Tr. as (1986) *Speed and Politics: An Essay on Dromology* (US: Semiotext).

Wakefield, M. 'Empire of the slum', *Spectator*, 18 August 2001, available at: http://www.spectator.co.uk/essays/9221/empire-of-the-slum.thtml (accessed 22 May 2010).

Weizman, E. (2006) 'Walking through walls: soldiers as architects in the Israeli–Palestinian conflict', *Radical Philosophy*, 136, pp. 8–22.

White, S.K. (1990) *The Recent Work of Jürgen Habermas: Reason, Justice and Modernity* (Cambridge: Cambridge University Press).

White, S.K. (1997) 'Reason, modernity and democracy', in S.K. White (ed.), *The Cambridge Companion to Habermas* (Cambridge: Cambridge University Press).

Wiener, N. (1948) *Cybernetics, or the Study of Control and Communication in the Animal and the Machine* (Cambridge, MA: The MIT Press).

Wolin, R. (1993) 'Introduction: total mobilisation', in R. Wolin (ed.), *The Heidegger Controversy: A Critical Reader* (Cambridge, MA: The MIT Press).

Wolin, R. (1994) 'Introduction', in Shierry Weber Nicholsen (ed.), *The New Conservatism: Cultural Criticism and the Historians' Debate* (Cambridge: Polity).

Wright, L. (2007) *The Looming Tower: Al-Qaeda's Road to 9/11* (London: Penguin).

Zielonka, J. (2000) *Enlargement and the Finality of European Integration*, Harvard Law School, available at: www.jeanmonnetprogram.org/papers/00/00F0801.rtf (accessed 24 July 2005).

Zolo, D. (1992) *Democracy and Complexity: A Realist Approach* (Cambridge: Polity).

Preface to the second edition

Arendt, H. (1951) *The Origins of Totalitarianism* (New York: Harcourt, Brace and Company).

Bailey, C. (2016) 'Democracy as Ideal and Practice: Historicizing *The Crisis of the European Union*', in G.M. Genna, T.O. Haakenson and I.W. Wilson (eds), *Jürgen Habermas and the European Economic Crisis: Cosmopolitanism Reconsidered* (Abingdon and New York: Routledge).

Ballard, J.G. (2006) *Kingdom Come* (London: Fourth Estate).

BBC News (2018) 'France Gilets Jaunes: Macron promises divide protest leaders', *BBC News: Europe*, 11 December 2018, available at: https://www.bbc.co.uk/news/world-europe-46522628 (accessed 12 December 2018).

Bolaño, R. (2004) *2666* (Barcelona: Editorial Anagrama). Tr. as (2009) *2666* (London: Picador).

Chakrabortty, A. (2016) 'Wolfgang Streeck: the German economist calling time on capitalism', *The Guardian*, 9 December 2016, available at: https://www.theguardian.com/books/2016/dec/09/wolfgang-streeck-the-german-economist-calling-time-on-capitalism (accessed 11 December 2018).

Eurointelligence (2018) 'A further move in Warsaw to submit to the ECJ's authority', *Eurointelligence Professional Daily Morning Briefing*, 31 October 2018, available at: https://www.eurointelligence.com/public/briefings/2018-10-31.html (accessed 12 December 2018).

Genna, G.M. and Wilson, I.W. (2016) 'Introduction: Europe at the Crossroads', in G.M. Genna, T.O. Haakenson and I.W. Wilson (eds), *Jürgen Habermas and the European Economic Crisis: Cosmopolitanism Reconsidered* (Abingdon and New York: Routledge).

Gray, J. (2016) 'The strange death of liberal politics', *New Statesman*, 5 July 2016, available at: https://www.newstatesman.com/politics/uk/2016/07/strange-death-liberal-politics (accessed 11 December 2018).

Habermas, J. (1968) *Erkenntnis und Interesse* (Frankfurt: Suhrkamp Verlag). Tr. as (1978) *Knowledge and Human Interests* (London: Heinemann).

Habermas, J. (2003) *The Future of Human Nature* (Cambridge: Polity).

Habermas, J. (2013) *Im Sog der Technokratie* (Berlin: Suhrkamp Verlag). Tr. as (2015) *The Lure of Technocracy* (Cambridge: Polity).

Habermas, J. (2013a) Erasmus Prize acceptance speech, available at: http://www.erasmus-prijs.org/prijswinnaars?itemid=53AFB450-04FC-1371-9AE18BB1978B2677&lang=en&mode=detail (accessed 12 December 2018).

Habermas, J. (2014) 'Internet and Public Sphere: What the Web Can't Do', *Reset DOC*, 24 July 2014, available at: https://www.resetdoc.org/story/internet-and-public-sphere-what-the-web-cant-do/ (accessed 12 December 2018).

Habermas, J. (2015a) *The Lure of Technocracy* (Cambridge: Polity).

Habermas, J. (2015b) 'Why Angela Merkel Is Wrong On Greece', *Social Europe*, 25 June 2015, available at: https://www.socialeurope.eu/why-angela-merkels-is-wrong-on-greece (accessed 12 December 2018).

Habermas, J. (2015c) Interview with Philip Oltermann, *The Guardian*, 16 July 2015, available at: https://www.theguardian.com/commentisfree/2015/jul/16/jurgen-habermas-eu-greece-debt-deal (accessed 12 December 2018).

Habermas, J. (2015d) 'Critique and communication: Philosophy's missions', *Eurozine*, 16 October 2015, available at: https://www.eurozine.com/critique-and-communication-philosophys-missions/?pdf (accessed 12 December 2018).

Habermas, J. (2015e) 'The Paris Attack And Its Aftermath', *Social Europe*, 26 November 2015, available at: https://www.socialeurope.eu/habermas-paris-attack (accessed 12 December 2018).

Habermas, J. (2016a) 'The players resign – Core Europe to the rescue: a conversation with Jürgen Habermas about Brexit and the EU crisis', *Zeit Online*, 12 July 2016, available at: https://www.zeit.de/kultur/2016-07/juergen-habermas-brexit-eu-crises-english (accessed 11 December 2018).

Habermas, J. (2016b) 'For A Democratic Polarisation: How To Pull The Ground From Under Right-wing Populism', *Social Europe*, 17 November 2016, available at: https://www.socialeurope.eu/democratic-polarisation-pull-ground-right-wing-populism (accessed 12 December 2018).

Habermas, J. (2017a) 'Citizen and State Equality in a Supranational Political Community: Degressive Proportionality and the *Pouvoir Constituant Mixte*', *Journal of Common Market Studies*, 55(2), pp. 171–182.

Habermas, J. (2017b) 'Why The Necessary Cooperation Does Not Happen: Introduction To A Conversation Between Emmanuel Macron and Sigmar Gabriel on Europe's Future', *Social Europe*, 20 March 2017, available at: https://www.socialeurope.eu/pulling-cart-mire-renewed-case-european-solidarity (accessed 12 December 2018).

Habermas, J. (2017c) 'What Macron Means for Europe: "How Much Will the Germans Have to Pay"', *Spiegel Online*, 26 October 2017, available at: http://www.spiegel.de/international/europe/juergen-habermas-on-the-european-vision-of-emmanuel-macron-a-1174721.html (accessed 12 December 2018).

Habermas, J. (2018a) 'For God's sake, spare us governing philosophers!', *El País*, 25 May 2018, available at: https://elpais.com/elpais/2018/05/07/inenglish/1525683618_1457 60.html (accessed 12 December 2018).

Habermas, J. (2018b) 'Are We Still Good Europeans?', *Zeit Online*, 6 July 2018, available at: https://www.zeit.de/kultur/2018-07/european-union-germany-challenges-loyalty-solidarity (accessed 12 December 2018).

Habermas, J. (2018c) '"New" Perspectives For Europe', *Social Europe*, 22 October 2018, available at: https://www.socialeurope.eu/new-perspectives-for-europe (accessed 13 December 2018).

Houellebecq, M. (1991) *H.P. Lovecraft : Contre le monde, contre la vie* (Monaco: Éditions du Rocher).

Houellebecq, M. (1998) *Les particules élémentaires* (Paris: Flammarion). Tr. as (2001) *Atomised* (London: Vintage).

Houellebecq, M. (2015) *Soumission* (Paris: Flammarion).

Humphreys, J. (2017) 'Paul Ricoeur: The philosopher behind Emmanuel Macron', *The Irish Times*, 30 May 2017, available at: https://www.irishtimes.com/culture/

paul-ricoeur-the-philosopher-behind-emmanuel-macron-1.3094792 (accessed 13 December 2018).

Kriss, S. (2017) 'The Sad Truth About Milo Yiannopoulos', *Vice*, 22 February 2017, available at: https://www.vice.com/en_uk/article/bmpjvv/the-sad-truth-about-milo-yiannopoulos (accessed 13 December 2018).

Lyotard, J.-F. (1979) *La Condition postmoderne: Rapport sur le savoir* (Paris: Minuit). Tr. as (1984) *The Postmodern Condition: A Report on Knowledge* (Minneapolis, MN: Minnesota University Press).

Macron, E. (2017) 'We Need to Develop Political Heroism', *Spiegel Online*, 13 October 2017, available at: http://www.spiegel.de/international/europe/interview-with-french-president-emmanuel-macron-a-1172745.html (accessed 11 December 2018).

Macron, E. (2018) Televised speech on the *gilets jaunes* protests, *L'Obs*, 10 December 2018, available at: https://www.youtube.com/watch?v=L9S_WF_YlkM (accessed 13 December 2018).

McLemee, S. (2011) 'From Culture War to Shooting War', *Inside Higher Ed*, 10 August 2011, available at: https://www.insidehighered.com/views/2011/08/10/culture-war-shooting-war (accessed 13 December 2018).

Outhwaite, W. (2017) 'Preface', in W. Outhwaite (ed.), *Brexit: Sociological Responses* (London and New York: Anthem Press).

Schmitt, C. (1922) *Politische Theologie: Vier Kapitel zur Lehre von der Souveränität* (Berlin: Duncker & Humblot). Tr. as (1985) *Political Theology: Four Chapters on the Concept of Sovereignty* (Cambridge, MA: The MIT Press).

Sloterdijk, P. (2016) 'Vom Unbehagen der Demokratie', *Die Zeit*, 24 November 2016.

Steiner, G. (1964) 'A Note on Günter Grass', in (1969) *Language and Silence: Essays 1958–1966* (London: Pelican).

Streeck, W. (2014) 'Small State Nostalgia? The Currency Union, Germany, and Europe: A Reply to Jürgen Habermas', *Constellations*, 21(2), pp. 213–221.

Streeck, W. (2017) 'What about capitalism? Jürgen Habermas's project of a European democracy', *European Political Science*, 16(2), pp. 246–253.

Tuymans, L. (2016) A discussion of the work of James Ensor, *Financial Times*, 28 October 2016, available at: https://www.youtube.com/watch?v=vQPmtvmA8-8 (accessed 11 December 2018).

Varoufakis, Y. (2017) 'Macron came to Greece's aid during our crisis. The French left should back him', *The Guardian*, 4 May 2017, available at: https://www.theguardian.com/commentisfree/2017/may/04/macron-greece-french-left-marine-le-pen-yanis-varoufakis (accessed 13 December 2018).

Varoufakis, Y. (2018) 'Our plan to revive Europe can succeed where Macron and Piketty failed', *The Guardian*, 13 December 2018, available at: https://www.theguardian.com/commentisfree/2018/dec/13/plan-europe-macron-piketty-green-new-deal-britain (accessed 18 December 2018).

Zuboff, S. (2019) 'Facebook, Google and a dark age of surveillance capitalism', *Financial Times*, 25 January 2019, available at: https://www.ft.com/content/7fafec06-1ea2-11e9-b126-46fc3ad87c65 (accessed 19 April 2019).

INDEX

Note: 'n' after a page reference indicates the number of a note on that page